# Organizational
# Communication

# INTERPERSONAL COMMTEXTS

**Series Editors: Mark L. Knapp & John A. Daly,**
*both at the University of Texas*

Designed for college and university undergraduates, the **Interpersonal Commtexts** series will also interest a much larger general audience. Ideal as basic or supplementary texts, these volumes are suited for courses in the development and practice of interpersonal skills; verbal and nonverbal behavior (the basis of interpersonal transactions); functions of communication in face-to-face interaction; the development of interpersonal behavior at various points in the lifespan; and intergroup and intercultural aspects of interpersonal communication. Readable and comprehensive, the **Interpersonal Commtexts** describe contexts within which interpersonal communication takes place and provide ways to study and understand the interpersonal communication process.

# Organizational Communication
## Connectedness in Action

Cynthia Stohl

INTERPERSONAL COMMTEXTS 5

**SAGE** Publications
*International Educational and Professional Publisher*
Thousand Oaks  London  New Delhi

*For information address:*

SAGE Publications, Inc.
2455 Teller Road
Thousand Oaks, California 91320
E-mail: order@sagepub.com

SAGE Publications Ltd.
6 Bonhill Street
London EC2A 4PU
United Kingdom

SAGE Publications India Pvt. Ltd.
M-32 Market
Greater Kailash I
New Delhi 110 048 India

Printed in the United States of America

**Library of Congress Cataloging-in-Publication Data**

Stohl, Cynthia.
    Organizational communication: Connectedness in action  /  Cynthia
Stohl.
      p.    cm. — (Interpersonal commtexts ; 5)
    Includes bibliographical references and index.
    ISBN 0-8039-3424-6 (cloth : acid-free paper). — ISBN
0-8039-3425-4 (pbk. : acid-free paper)
    1. Communication in organizations.    2. Interpersonal
communication.    I. Title.    II. Series.
    HD30.3.S758    1995
    658.4′5—dc20                                                                95-2521

This book is printed on acid-free paper.

96  97  98  99  00  01  10  9  8  7  6  5  4  3  2

Sage Production Editor:  Astrid Virding
Typesetter:  Janelle LeMaster

# Contents

# Part II: The Complex Matrix

# Part III: Linking Communication and Organization

*In loving memory of my father, Jack,*
*and my brother, Jerry . . .*
*their voices remain beautiful and strong.*

# *Preface*

The purpose of this book is to use a network perspective to help build bridges and links that have been missing in most traditional textbooks. This text provides a new formulation of organizational networks, focusing upon *connectedness* and *collaborative* interaction. The network metaphor captures the richness, complexity, and fragmentation of contemporary organizations and highlights the connections among experiences in and outside the workplace. The text is intended to provide the following:

(1) *A link between interpersonal and organizational communication.* Most texts and research focus on either the world of work or the world of non-work. Divergent perspectives have led to mutually exclusive domains of understanding. Yet as the vast changes in the American family, social structure, and global economy suggest, these are not independent fields of experience. The boundaries among home life, social life, and work life have always been blurred and permeable; contemporary experience brings these embedded relationships to the fore. This book is

designed to be a supplement but not a comprehensive text of either area.

> *Increasing globalization has made extended international experience a prerequisite for advancement in many organizations. The stresses and successes experienced by employees' families living abroad are strongly associated with expatriate employees' positive assimilation and effective work performance.*

(2) *A link for understanding the intimate relationship between experiences in and outside the workplace.* Organizational reality is guided by our culture, our direct/indirect and internal/external affiliations. Individual behavior can be best understood socially; each of us stands at the nexus of a multitude of constraining alignments. It is our network of relationships that helps determine our values, attitudes, ideas, perceptions, and experience of work.

> *The reaction to a request for overtime will vary depending upon one's personal situation: If a child is going off to college, the extra income may be welcomed; if the child is in school, the cost of day care may offset any gains from overtime; if the employee is newly in love, the necessity to cancel the weekend getaway may be extremely costly.*

(3) *A link between contemporary organizational events and communication concepts.* Modern organizations have resolved many problems and afforded new opportunities. To understand the new resolutions and dilemmas of life in organizational America, we must examine the central role of communication.

> *Substance abuse programs for employees, provision of day care, career planning, and so on are becoming commonplace organizational practices. Issues of confidentiality and privacy are just two of the communicative concerns such programs bring to the fore.*

(4) *A link for understanding the relationship between communication processes and the potential empowerment of individuals.* Through communication we evolve our culture, our social struc-

tures, and our worldviews. Communication also shapes our perceptions of what is and what could be. The foundation of all social relationships is communicative; the power of transforming relationships is communicative as well.

*Class action suits, often designed to alter specific communicative practices within organizations, typically grow out of informal linkages that facilitate shared perceptions and a collective view of experience. Only when women talk to one another outside the official channels may they discover their low salaries are not indicative of individual capabilities but reflect a systematic bias in the organization.*

## ❏ Summary

This book focuses upon the multileveled interfaces between organizational and interpersonal domains. Neither work life nor personal life can be known, or experienced, to the exclusion of the other. Each of us is enmeshed in a unique network of relationships and identifications that permeate, constrain, and facilitate our organizational experience. It is the goal of this text to highlight these linkages as we explore the processes of organizational communication.

# Acknowledgments

This book is about the fundamental importance of connections and the collaborative nature of organizing and knowing. From this perspective it is clearly impossible to acknowledge all who have influenced my ways of thinking and viewing the world. I am very fortunate to have such a rich and vibrant network of family, friends, colleagues, and students.

There are, however, several "links" who deserve special recognition. My organizational communication colleagues at Purdue, both past and present—George Cheney, Louis Cusella, Robin Clair, Alicia Marshall, Dennis Mumby, Linda Putnam, Charles Redding, Ruth Smith, Sandi Smith, Elaine Tompkins, and Phillip Tompkins—have blurred traditional distinctions among friends, colleagues, and teachers. Their collective wisdom and good humor have contributed greatly to my life and my work. My wonderful conversations and association with Benedicte Madsen at the University of Århus, Denmark also played an important role in the development of the ideas in this book. Of course, I, alone, am responsible for what I have produced here. I especially do want, however, to acknowledge the contributions of Susan Schell in the early stages of this project. I am also most thankful for the help of the series editors, Mark Knapp and John Daly at the University of Texas, and the efforts of Sophy Craze and Astrid Virding of Sage Publications.

As this book illustrates, we cannot separate our work from our personal lives. Most significantly, my mother Sylvia's indomitable spirit permeates my entire family and all that we may accomplish. My remarkable daughters, Rachel and Ilene, have given me support and love in ways that continually amaze and delight me. They connect me to a world that will be better because of who and what they are. And finally I want to acknowledge the loving and sustaining contributions of my husband, Michael, to all aspects of my intellectual and emotional life. Only he (and perhaps not even he) can ever know or appreciate all that he has given me in the past, the present, and for our future together.

# PART I

# Organizations as Networks

# Connectedness in Action

On any given day, of any given week, it is likely that you have communicated in and been influenced by dozens of organizations. Organizations are so pervasive in modern life that we often do not notice our daily associations within these cooperative systems.

- Most of us "go to the doctor" barely cognizant of the fact that our doctor is part of a huge clinical practice controlling and coordinating the activities of dozens of doctors, nurses, technicians, clerks, maintenance workers, accountants, and public relations people. Yet these linkages strongly affect the communication that takes place in the doctor's office.
- As we enter our local department store, we give little, if any, thought to the fact that our purchases are being framed by literally thousands of international and organizational linkages. Nonetheless, multinational connections may determine the actual items available for sale, international marketing efforts influence our tastes and desires, global competition shapes quality

3

control processes, and worldwide human resource consultants
fashion the character of the employee service we receive.

• University students are usually too preoccupied with friends,
fraternities, football, and finishing course assignments to give
much attention to their connections to fiscal planning, physical
plant, and purchasing departments. These systems, however, are
all fundamental units of complex universities and are part of
the communicative climate that helps shape our interactions on
campus.

• When employees go home from a day's work, despite their
best intentions, they cannot leave their organizational connections at the office. What people talk about and how they talk
about issues are influenced by their communicative affiliations
in the workplace.

The focus of this book is on organizational communication, but
it takes as its starting point the idea that to understand organizational communication we must pay close attention to the linkages
individuals develop and maintain both as a part of and apart
from each organizational context. Our personal lives and our
views of the world are intricately interwoven with our work
relations and our organizational perspective. In this text, *organizational communication* is defined as *the collective and interactive
process of generating and interpreting messages*. Networks of understanding are created through coordinated activities and relationships that permeate organizational boundaries.

In their book *Organizational America*, Scott and Hart (1979)
advance the thesis that America's most successful invention may
be the modern organization with its subtle but profound influence on American values and American life. Certainly, as Americans have faced difficult times, we have looked to our organizations both as the source of problems and as the best hope for
solutions. Our sudden loss of competitive advantage is blamed
on schools that don't educate students to be quality workers,
factories that operate with antiquated and inefficient communication technologies, and bureaucracies that bury managers in red
tape. Simultaneously, we look for solutions in "new partnerships" and the development of networks among business and

industry, education, and government. These answers increasingly blur the taken-for-granted distinctions between organizational and interpersonal experiences and obscure the boundaries among local, national, and global spheres of influence.

The belief that our personal and work lives operate independently of each other, often referred to as the "myth of separate worlds" (Kanter, 1977), has persisted since industrialization. The Protestant ethic, deeply ingrained in American culture, reinforced the expectation that we were to "act as though" we had no commitment beyond the workplace. "Relevant" communication was bounded within an organization's borders.

But private and work lives are more diffuse than distinct. It is impossible to separate these arenas of activity. After you graduate from college and establish a career, for example, you may be expected to serve your company by being involved in civic organizations, joining the school board, or becoming active in some type of social service. Clearly, these types of involvement affect your communication both privately and publicly. If you are promoted, you may expect to move to a better neighborhood and forge new social connections. If your company announces that it may have to lay off workers, the message has several interpersonal ramifications. Significantly, stable employment creates stable families just as unemployment creates social problems. High rates of alcoholism are linked to certain job characteristics and physical ailments are correlated with certain jobs (Voydanoff, 1984). As early as 1964, researchers found that nearly a third of American males were disturbed by the extent to which their jobs interfered with their family lives (Kahn, Wolfe, Quinn, Snoek, & Rosenthal, 1964).

As long as American organizations were healthy and successful, however, these embedded relationships were considered beyond the purview of most organizational researchers, consultants, and management. Organizational communication was conceived as a bounded, linear process that took place within a particular context (Katz & Kahn, 1966).

But contemporary events have forced us to rethink this container view of organizational communication (Smith, 1993). Organizations are challenged by global competition. Direct foreign investment in U.S. corporations is increasing at a rate of over 20% per year (Glickman & Woodward, 1989). Communication technologies link employees who are separated by thousands of miles and several time zones creating organizations whose members do not share a similar space, may never see one another, and are culturally diverse. In other words, organizational environments are becoming more interconnected and more complicated. According to the "law of requisite variety" (Weick, 1979), organizations, to survive, must develop complexity equivalent to the diversity of their interactive environments. In the 1990s, organizational communication is taking on greater and greater degrees of flexibility, diffusion of function, and diversity of meaning. This sense of fragmentation and loss of stable boundaries typifies scholars' conceptions of what are called postmodern organizations (Clegg, 1990).

> *Organizational environments are becoming more interconnected and more complicated.*

Consider, for a moment, the communicative implications of the Hudson report *Workforce 2000*. This influential report documents the increasing diversity of organizational experience. Only 7% of families today fit the traditional model of a husband working outside the home, the wife at home, and two school-age children. More and more women and minorities are entering the workforce, over 10 million mothers of preschoolers are pursuing careers, and more than half the mothers of children under 6 years old work. By the year 2000, the American workforce is expected to be gender balanced. At the end of this century, the report projects that only 58% of the new entrants into the labor force will be "white native Americans," 22% are expected to be immigrants, and the remaining 20% will be African Americans and Hispanic Americans. Paradoxically, as American workers are becoming more educated, 65% of the workforce reads below the ninth-grade level (Johnston & Packer, 1987).

These changing demographic characteristics directly affect organizational communication in several ways. For example, scholars suggest that after 3:00 p.m. some single parents' productivity goes down because family issues become the focus of many discussions on the work floor, time is less efficiently spent as phone calls from home may interrupt the work flow, and efforts to activate a support network take away from efforts directed toward the work task (Sullivan, 1981). Thus organizations are attempting to become "more family friendly" by providing benefits and developing programs to help solve family problems that spill over into the workplace.

A survey released in 1992 by the Conference Board ("CEO Survey," 1992), a non-profit business research organization, indicated that 45% of the top 180 U.S. organizations (e.g., IBM Corporation, Corning Glass, Marriott, Xerox, Cummins, Levi Strauss, and Pepsico) are developing flexible work-family programs. Flex benefits enable workers to decide how to allocate benefits among dental and medical programs, child or elderly care. Flextime allows workers to decide what type of work schedule is best for them, their families, and their organizations. Employee assistance programs provide professional counseling and psychotherapy for a number of personal problems including drug addiction, alcoholism, obesity, bereavement, and family violence. Management hopes the resultant changes in employees' communication behavior and increases in productivity will offset the cost of such services.

In response to the decreasing skill level of many new employees, American organizations have also taken on additional functions. Continuing education no longer remains the province of the public education system and universities. Like their Japanese counterparts, who for more than four decades have been directly involved in employee education, companies such as Goodyear, Motorola, Eastman Chemical, and Hewlett Packard have developed literacy and remedial classes in basic math and science skills for their workforce (Jackson, 1992). In these expanded contexts, teachers become co-workers and supervisors become students; organizational communication changes because relationships change.

Overall, employee benefits and working conditions have taken on greater flexibility as human resource experts become more and more aware of the reciprocal influences between interpersonal and organizational communication. Many scholars and practitioners suggest these benefits empower workers and function to improve the quality of working life. Other researchers, who operate from what is called a "critical perspective," warn that "benefits" of this type are "golden handcuffs" that control

### MAKING CONNECTIONS

The traditional assumption that once employees enter the workplace all social roles except that of worker become irrelevant is outdated. Today's workforce encompasses more women, minorities, elderly, and dual-career couples. Thus the "myth of separate worlds" can no longer be perpetuated without serious problems for both employers and employees. Working parents do not forget their sick child home in bed when they get to work, custodial fathers are aware that the demanded overtime is conflicting with child care arrangements, and workers with elderly parents and little extended family are fully cognizant of the potential difficulties associated with geographic relocation. Modern organizations are just beginning to confront the multiple roles that their employees face and some are beginning to help employees define and manage boundaries as well as make these boundaries more flexible. Many U.S. firms provide some form of family benefits.

United Services Automobile Association employs over 13,000 employees and is exemplary of the new type of American corporation that recognizes the linkage between home and work lives. As you read their list of benefits, consider how communication within this company and employee communication outside the work environment may be affected as employees use these opportunities. Available benefits include the following:

child care
tennis courts
a company store
lighted softball fields
a well-stocked library
a physical fitness center
annual checkups after age 50
jogging trails and picnic groves
a lake stocked with perch and trout
clinic staffed with nine registered nurses
buying service for cars, jewelry, and furniture
subsidized "dump your plump" cafeteria meals
college courses given in 60 classrooms on the premises
a food takeout service for working couples and single parents
a subsidized van pool transporting workers from distances up to 60 miles
access to 13 professional psychotherapeutic counselors to deal with personal and family problems

workers' attitudes and communication to a far greater extent than the traditional authoritarian styles of management. It is important to note that, as different as these functional and critical perspectives may be, each underscores that organizational reality is guided by our internal and external affiliations.

The introduction of new technologies into the workplace also affects the complexity of organizational communication processes. Workers may no longer be situated in the same space or time as their supervisors and co-workers. The advent of personal computers is enabling many workers to do much of their work at home. Portable telephones, modems, fax machines, and beepers can be used anywhere and at any time. Teleconferencing and electronic mail services transcend office walls. The need to speak immediately with a colleague in Singapore after receiving a FAX at 2 a.m. (eastern standard time) on Thursday (2 p.m. Friday in Singapore) precludes regular 9 to 5 workdays. Under these conditions, the traditional forms of management-worker communication become irrelevant as well as ineffective. Moreover, when workers are no longer simultaneously at the work site, there is less overlap and interaction among specializations, people are less identified with the organization, and co-workers are not available for social and task support.

The "myth of separate worlds" is clearly a fiction that perpetuates an outdated bounded view of organizational life. To understand organizational communication, we need to acquire and develop tools of analysis that let us "unpack" the myriad, complex, and overlapping activities that constitute organizational life. The next section introduces one tool that is essential in our search for understanding—the organizational metaphor.

## ❏ Organizational Metaphors

Most of us probably first encountered the *metaphor* in an English class where it was defined as "the application of a word or phrase to an object or concept it does not literally denote" (*American Heritage Dictionary*, 1978). Poets, we all learned, delight in metaphors ("The fog crept in on little cat's feet"); phrase makers rely on them ("Life is just a bowl of cherries"); playwrights exploit them (*Cat on a Hot Tin Roof*); and news correspondents mix them ("But scab labor is a cynic's marketplace: Brought in on a whisper and dangled like fish bait, they inherit the wind" (Tony Korneheiser, 1987, *Washington Post*, reprinted by permission, reported in "Block That Metaphor," 1987, p. 50).

But metaphors are also a commonplace of everyday language use. The essence of metaphor, Lakoff and Johnson (1980) write in *Metaphors We Live By*, is understanding and experiencing one kind of thing in terms of another. For example, we can understand more about North Americans' concept of time through the metaphorical concept: Time is money. Looking at several common phrases used in relation to time: *"You're wasting my time." "This will save you hours." "I don't have the time to give you." "How do you spend your time these days?"*

> The essence of metaphor is understanding and experiencing one thing in terms of another.

Lakoff and Johnson reveal time to be a valuable and limited resource just like money. These metaphorical messages reproduce the typical North American's attitude that time is linear and material, a "real" thing that can be lost, saved, and divided. Edward Hall (1980), an anthropologist who has written several books on culture and how it affects communication practices of organizations throughout the world, contrasts Americans' monochronic perspective with a polychronic view. A monochronic culture views time as something that is material and substantial. Monochronic organizations compartmentalize functions and people, focus on punctuality and deadlines, and are most comfortable dealing with one thing at a time. In a polychronic organization (such as in the Latin cultures of South America), time is intangible. In these organizations, schedules are not nearly as important or rigidly adhered to, business people do not sequence meetings or activities in a linear fashion, and people are involved with many things at once.

Just as the way we talk about time influences our experience of time, the way we talk about organizational communication often presupposes metaphors that we may not be consciously aware of yet frame our understanding and experience of organizations. The conduit or pipeline metaphor of communication, for example, allows us to think communication is very easy and can be effective simply by making sure we are clear when we send a message (Axley, 1984).

Organizational metaphors emphasize certain perceptions, interpretations, and actions of organizing while deemphasizing others. To use a metaphor, some elements of our experiences are placed in the foreground while others are relegated to the background; each metaphor provides us with a different way of "seeing" organizational reality. If we "sec" our office group as a traditional family, then we expect people to take care of and protect one another. Within our group, dominant behavior would

---

**MAKING CONNECTIONS**

One of the primary differences among social science disciplines is the type of metaphor used to understand the social world. As the incident below indicates, our metaphors control not only what we see but the answers we find.

In the 1950s, a team of social scientists studied U.N. deliberations regarding the Middle East. Their data suggested that the ambassador from Ireland was playing a significant role in the formal and informal negotiations. The study group found his participation to be unexpected and puzzling. Thus they asked the question: What was the "connection" among the countries that could explain the Irish ambassador's involvement?

Each scientist, of course, operated from within his or her own paradigm and the metaphor associated with it. The connection was interpreted from his or her own view of what constituted a connection. The economist looked for economic "ties" between Ireland and the Middle East and found few of any magnitude; the political scientist looked to the treaties and alliances "binding" Ireland to the Middle East, and there was slight evidence for this; the historian looked to past events "linking" these countries together—very few. Finally, someone who saw connection as communication links made the following observation: In the United Nations, delegates are seated alphabetically, according to country. There were Iran, Iraq, Ireland, Israel, and, a few seats away, Jordan and Kuwait. The Irish delegate was embedded in a cluster that contained the leading actors in the drama; he was a key link in the chain! Thus the connection was found, the explanation made, and the importance of informal/emergent communication structures affirmed (see Alger, 1965, cited in Stohl, 1989b).

be interpreted as fatherly or motherly, the less competent or weaker members would be treated as children, with fewer rights but much support. Our personal lives would be appropriate topics for discussion and rituals surrounding birthdays, the birth of a child, and other personal landmarks would be enacted. If we "see" our work group as an army combat unit, we still expect people to protect one another but now against an outside enemy. Dominant members would be seen as leaders whose authority was unquestioned. The weaker members would be seen as liabilities who need to be replaced with stronger members. As the group "attacked" problems, personal concerns would have no place in the discourse. Rituals associated with successful assaults would be created, a celebration of a child's success would be inappropriate.

Metaphors are complex images and may evoke several different connotations. There is a great difference, for example, between using the family metaphor to describe the instrumental and expressive communication within the organization as in the example above, and invoking the family metaphor to describe the detached orientation of a company as the employee below suggests when contrasting the old place he worked for with his new place of employment: "They used to have a local tavern that was the company meeting place. All the men used to stop off for a drink after work. At [present 'family' company] no one does that—everyone goes home after work. They're much more family oriented" (Davis, 1982, p. 59).

In his book *Images of Organizations*, Gareth Morgan (1986) explores the dominant metaphors embedded in our contemporary theories and explanations of organizational experience, arguing that each metaphor leads "us to see and understand organizations in distinctive yet partial ways" (p. 13). Among the metaphors Morgan explores are organizations as *machines, living systems, brains, cultures, political systems,* and *instruments of domination.* None of these metaphors tells us everything there is to know about organizations, but each tells us something unique about organizations and organizational communication.

Each of the metaphors Morgan explicates highlights specific aspects of organizational experience, and facilitates what Morgan describes as "the art of reading and understanding organizations" (p. 12). Each metaphor encompasses a different way of thinking about and seeing organizations. Each metaphor has strengths and weaknesses; each highlights different aspects of organizational action.

> *Metaphors encompass different ways of thinking about and seeing organizations.*

The *machine* metaphor, for example, emphasizes those aspects of organizational experience that are *predictable, controllable,* and *reproducible.* Like machine parts, members fulfill *specific functions for the organization* and these parts are expected to take priority over any other functions they may serve. The "individual" plays only a supporting role as one of the many mechanical gadgets in the larger mechanism. Ackoff (1974) notes how the legitimation of the "organization as machine" in the first half of the twentieth century had far-reaching implications for how we viewed the relationships between home and work lives:

> Private life [of managers] ceased to exist apart from company life. The higher a man went, the more responsibility and hence, less freedom to live by . . . family life became just another cog in the corporate machine. (p. 34, quoting E. Jennings)

It is not surprising, in this view, that communication is viewed as bounded and instrumental. Communication is a straightforward process that directly transfers meaning from one person to another. Communication serves a command function for the organization; tightly controlled "orders" and "directives" are issued through "proper channels" to be executed by willing subordinates (Krone, Jablin, & Putnam, 1987).

Although the machine metaphor still dominates organizational imagery, as early as 1813, social visionaries such as Robert Owen attempted to energize management thinking by enlivening their mechanistic view of organizations. In an eloquent address to the superintendents of manufacturing, Owen suggested that

---

### MAKING CONNECTIONS

The machine metaphor is closely associated with the work of a classical organizational theorist, *Frederick Taylor*. Writing in the early 1900s, Taylor (1911/1947) attempted to apply the methods of science to the increasingly complex problems of control facing industrial organizations. His theory of *scientific management* incorporates several fundamental and mechanistic assumptions, including the following:

1. Through scientific analysis, management can find the one best way to perform a job. The scientific redesign of jobs is done through time and motion studies, which break down tasks into mechanistic parts and then identify the ways to minimize the actions necessary to complete the task. Once workers share their "rules of thumb" with management during the initial stage of job analysis, they are expected to carry out their jobs in the precise way prescribed by management.
2. Personnel should be chosen and trained scientifically according to specific characteristics that are necessary to do the job.
3. Productivity and workers' compensation should be directly related.
4. Each person may have multiple supervisors, "functional foremen," depending on the characteristics of his or her task in the production process. Relationships outside the work environment are irrelevant.

Charlie Chaplin's film classic *Modern Times* (1936) chillingly portrays the dehumanizing consequences of scientific management techniques. Ruled by demands for productivity and efficiency, we see workers treated as cogs in a machine. Social interactions are forbidden and the employee's actions are monitored continually. When Chaplin's character begins to fall behind on the production line, there is no way for him to stop its continuing demands. He falls into the machine and we watch him literally become part of the machine, eventually spewed out as just another object. The satirical presentation of the implications of management's mechanistic view of workers and organizations includes the introduction of a worker-feeding machine (to make eating more efficient and thereby save time). The hapless Chaplin is even watched on a large screen when he goes to the bathroom during a break to have a cigarette. Although an extraordinarily humorous parody of life in a manufacturing plant, *Modern Times* seriously delineates the consequences of using the machine metaphor.

Throughout the text, there are several "Making Connections" boxes that discuss the contributions of key figures in organizational theory. These scholars have had a powerful impact on the way researchers, managers, and employees understand organizational communication. As you read the summary of each theorist, consider what metaphor he or she seems to apply for understanding organizational communication.

the entire workforce, combined with the physical plant and equipment should be regarded as a system composed of many parts and . . . that it would be both morally right and financially advantageous if factory owners would pay as careful attention to the "more delicate complex living mechanism" as they customarily bestowed upon inanimate machines. (Robert Owen, 1813, in Merrill, 1960, pp. 11-15)

Owen's utopian vision has not been the focus of much systemic thinking in the contemporary world. Most commonly, when organizations are considered *living organisms*, attention is directed to the interdependent processes that allow a *system* to survive in the economic environment. The metaphor addresses the technical complexity of organizations but does not address emotional/social complexity (Mitroff, 1987). The systems metaphor associated with the image of living organisms views organizations as wholes with irreducible characteristics (the principle of *non-summativity*), which maintain themselves *(homeostasis)* through feedback, adjustment, and exchange with their environments *(open systems)*. The organization receives *inputs* from the environment and returns energy, information, and manufactured products or services *(outputs)*. There are several paths an organization may take that lead to the same end point *(equifinality)*.

The *brain* metaphor highlights the *information processing* aspects of organizations. The mind/body split is central to this view and creates a world in which the organization is seen as the center of *rationality* (brain) separate from the body, which is the center of nurturance and sustenance. Organizational communication is associated with the amount of *uncertainty* and types of information processing that are necessary.

Unlike the mechanical and organic metaphors that place primary emphasis on the structure and function of organizational processes, the cultural metaphor "sees" organized activity as *language, folklore, ceremonies*, and other social practices that communicate key ideologies, values, and beliefs. Viewing organizations as cultures highlights the symbolic significance of organizational activities. The cultural metaphor focuses upon people's *interpretations* of action and the collective meanings associated with particular activities. Many best-selling management texts in the 1980s used features of culture, such as *rites* (e.g., an induction ceremony for new employees), *rituals* (e.g., a company's Fourth of July picnic), *myths* (e.g., the narrative everyone knows of the company's founding), and *stories* (e.g., the everyday stories that employees tell one another that incorporate the company's values) to explain organizational behavior and develop strategies for making an organization more productive (Deal & Kennedy, 1982; Peters & Waterman, 1982).

The metaphor of organizations as *political systems* makes explicit what many experience but few talk about: organizational activity based on *self-interest*. All organizational communication has political dimensions and overtones. This metaphor draws attention to the *role of power* in determining organizational and hence political outcomes. From this perspective, *rationality, efficiency,* and *effectiveness* are value-laden terms whose meanings are always interest based. Unlike many of the metaphors, which

---

## MAKING CONNECTIONS

*Ian Mitroff* (1987), in a provocative book titled *Business* Not *as Usual,* argues that the political economic environment of the 1980s-1990s requires new organizing assumptions and hence new metaphors. He suggests that even the complex system theories that replaced mechanistic views and have come to dominate organizational thinking are too rational and mechanical to "fit" the competitive, volatile, diverse, globalized marketplace.

The first alternative metaphor Mitroff presents is "The World as a Complex Hologram." This view emphasizes organizational complexity and interdependence. Mitroff highlights a fundamental part of the hologram. That is, if part of a hologram is enlarged, the result is not merely an enlargement of that part; it is a fuzzy picture of the whole hologram. When we understand organizations as holograms, we "see" that the *whole is contained in every part of the organization although not to the same degree of clarity.* Thus individual employees and their relationships are not merely economic, rational events, they include the psychodynamic needs, identifications, and dreams of the individuals. Transactions operate on many more levels and are far more complex than they appear.

Mitroff's second metaphor, "The World as a Global Garden," presents a powerful image that can help us understand the success of Japanese organizational structures such as "just in time inventory," systems of quality control, and societal institutions such as the Ministry of International Trade and Industry (the system credited with responsibility for Japanese economic achievements since World War II). Aesthetics is a

*(continued)*

view organizations as functionally integrated systems, the political metaphor emphasizes *diversity of interests* and *fragmented goals*. "Seeing" organizations as *instruments of domination* further refines the political nature of organizations and is compatible with both critical and feminist theory. This metaphor focuses on the ways in which the *interests of the dominant group* (e.g., employers, males) are forcefully and unobtrusively maintained over the interests of the less powerful. From this view, we can see how organizational structure and discourse systematically *privilege* some and *oppress* many organizational actors.

Overall, Morgan's metaphor analyses present us with a rich and complex understanding of organizations. Each is instructive and insightful, yet each is limited and flawed. Every metaphor highlights and "hides" certain things. Throughout this book, the *network* metaphor is used because it leads us to conceptualize our organizational experiences with an emphasis on *connectedness*

---

predominant value in Japanese culture and the concept of the garden, according to Mitroff, represents the deepest expression of Japanese aesthetics. Basic tenets of Japanese gardening include the following:

1. Nature is symbolized and represented, not imitated.
2. Straight lines and perfect geometric shapes are rarely used—nature is not conceived as an orderly, precise machine.
3. Asymmetrical designs and odd numbers of groupings are preferred.
4. Contrast is important, as is fluidity and change.
5. Everything superfluous to the total effect of the garden is discarded.
6. The garden does not have a single view; each view appears as one walks around and within it.
7. The gardener is concerned with the interaction of every part—shapes, colors, slopes, sounds, and so on.
8. Every stone, tree, plant has a particular shape and a will of its own, but master gardeners know how to coax and humor these willful stones into submission.
9. Too strict adherence to forms and inflexible design is equivalent in the words of an old Japanese proverb to straightening the horns and killing the cow.

It is important to note that Mitroff is not claiming that the Japanese have explicitly or deliberately used the concept of a garden in the design of their factories, compensation systems, treatment of employees, or the environment. "But," he writes, "there is an uncanny parallel. . . . Is it really any surprise to find a preoccupation with quality in a society that places such emphasis on the value of individual stones?" (p. 179).

and the central role played by *communication*. Networks span
boundaries. Organizations as networks captures the tapestry of
*relationships*—the complex web of *affiliations* among individuals
and organizations as they are woven through the collaborative
threads of communication. The network consists of *interconnected*
individuals who are linked by *patterned* flows of information,
influence, and affect both within and across organizational
boundaries. A network perspective enables us to incorporate and
extend conventional notions of structure and focus upon the
complex, dynamic, interwoven fabric of social affiliations. Instead of finding answers in the attributes of individuals, histories, or institutions, we will look for our answers in the attributes
of relationships—people known, the nature of their bonds, the
extent of interconnectedness, and so forth.

## ❑ Final Connections

The network metaphor encapsulates the full range of potential systems of organizing. The most traditional bureaucratic
organization in Washington, D.C., or a workers' cooperative in
Mondragon, Spain, can be conceived in network terms. "Organizations as networks" gives us a conscious alternative to top-
down, hierarchical organizations. Networks can be centralized
or decentralized, adaptive or inflexible, segmented or integrated
systems with single or multiple leaders. A network may be consciously created to gain position and power and yet its structure
may promote cooperation, equality, and harmony. "Networks are
systems of exchange and integration rather than violence and
coercion" (Mulgan, 1991, p. 21).

When we consider the transformative and empowering nature
of network imagery, it is not surprising that social action associations such as TRANET (Transnational Appropriate/Alternative
Technology Network) and the National Women's Health Network, professional organizations like Networking 108 (a group
of over 100 international journalists who share ideas and resources at monthly meetings), and self-help groups such as the

Office for Open Networks of Pattern Research in Denver, Colorado (which helps people find others who have resources they need) and the Displaced Homemakers Network have incorporated the network image into their names.

The appropriateness of the metaphor "organizations as networks" corresponds to other cultural turns of the 1990s. Many view networks as the quintessential organizational form of the postindustrial, information society (Mulgan, 1991). Naisbitt and Aburdene (1990) cite the shift from hierarchy to networks as one of the 10 megatrends shaping the future. They write: "We are giving up dependence on hierarchical structures in favor of informal networks" (p. 12). As a verb, *networking* has entered our language to mean making connections among peers. As a noun, *network* describes all types of social systems, especially organizations that link people with shared values and interests. In *The Networking Book*, Lipnack and Stamps (1986) note that

> *Many view networks as the quintessential organizational form of the postindustrial, information society.*

> while classic "old boy" networks have held things in check for centuries with their limited view of the meaning of "we," in recent years networking has opened up new lines of communication both locally and globally. . . . Whereas once charts of pyramiding boxes were believed to be the only rational map by which people organize themselves, today systems of intertwining, densely populated networks can be found supplementing, weaving through and sometimes totally eclipsing hierarchies. (p. 3)

The network metaphor, rich and multitextured, draws to our attention several organizational paradoxes we will encounter throughout this text. For example, this chapter indicates that *networks are stable and ever changing* and *networks are powerful organizational structures that are constituted and reconstituted through interpersonal communication*. It is the recognition of and involvement with the paradoxical nature of organizational life that enables and empowers us to go forward and change the systems that we create.

# A Network Perspective

*The first chapter expanded our view of organizational communication beyond the metaphors in which it has been traditionally framed. This chapter further illuminates the network metaphor and focuses upon the dynamic interplay between individuals and social systems.*

The "organization as network" is an intuitively appealing metaphor. It focuses upon the intricate patterns of relationships that constitute complex systems. A network embodies the powerful image of an interconnected world. Communication in a "network" organization is often touted as the exemplar for organizational innovation in our globalized economy (Mulgan, 1991). Organizational activities are easily conceived in network terms; there are conferences, support groups, and books specifically designed to teach people how "to network effectively" (Smith, 1984). A recent keynote speech to the Society of Professional

Management Consultants was even titled "Social and Professional Networking Vital to Survival of Institutions" (Lipnack & Stamps, 1986).

Consider the typical geographic small talk you hear at social functions, "Oh, you're from New York, do you know . . .?" the name dropping practiced in offices everywhere, and the proverbial and often repeated comment, "It's not what you know, but who you know." These commonplace messages recognize the potential power of network linkages and are consistent with the "moral" of several well-known organizational stories. For example, automobile industry insiders suggest that "Lee A. Iacocca was ousted from the Ford Motor Company's presidency because he failed, in Henry Ford's view, to develop support through presence and grace and social relationships" (Kadushin, 1978, p. A19). In contrast, the story goes, Philip Caldwell, his successor, had nurtured the appropriate connections. Caldwell's professional and social contacts were among the 47 highly interconnected people who were believed to run Detroit (Tichy, 1981). John J. McCloy, who during his lifetime was chairman of the Rockefeller Foundation, the Ford Foundation, and the Chase Manhattan Bank, President of the World Bank, and named in *The Power Elite* (Mills, 1957) as part of America's "inner core," enjoyed telling the story of how as a young college student he "walked up to the door of the Rockefeller mansion . . . and asked for a job, the butler slammed the door in his face." Soon after, McCloy recalls, "he managed to secure a position teaching sailing to the Rockefeller children, including Nelson and David, both of whom were later central to his career" (Finder, 1992, p. 23. Copyright © 1992 by The New York Times Company. Reprinted by permission).

The story of Mary Cunningham, the highly competent Bendix executive who was accused of "sleeping her way to the top," exemplifies the sometimes dangerous and often destructive power of network attributions. Ironically, in the workplace, when "outsiders" threaten the status quo, they often become targets of negative stereotypes that equate their success with who they know rather than their job capabilities and performance.

## ❑ Networks: Organizations as Connectedness in Action

What does it mean when we say that we will use a network metaphor to help us see and understand organizational communication? To begin, organizations are seen as *connectedness in action*, an endless series of textured relationships that move into and influence one another (Cooper & Fox, 1990). An organizational network therefore is much more than a "communication structure" or an "information flowchart." It is the tapestry of communicative relationships, a complex, interwoven, symbolic fabric. Networks capture the degree to which a system may be

---

### MAKING CONNECTIONS

The seductive power of network connections is exemplified in the two news stories excerpted below. Both Larry Smith and David Bloom attempted to capitalize on people's desire to be associated with, and their willingness to trust, those "in the know."

In August 1989 the National Republican Senatorial Committee sent a letter signed by President Bush congratulating Larry Smith and 50,000 other Americans on being accepted into the Republican Senatorial Inner Circle. This letter was followed up with another letter asking members to send in $1,000. In return, the letter promised the individual could receive personal briefings with members of the Cabinet, senior White House aides, and several Republican senators.

Smith sent in his $1,000 and then immediately sent letters to large corporations claiming to be part of the Washington "inner circle" and promising them access to top political figures. According to the Washington Post, Mr. Smith's lobbying fee ranged from $1,000 to $4,000. We do not know if anyone actually hired Smith before the ruse was detected but there is evidence that his membership in the Inner Circle was revoked ("The Short Run," 1990, p. 4. This material appeared in *Dollars and Sense*, a popular economics magazine. Subscription $18.95 from *D&S*, 1 Summer St., Somerville, MA 02143).

In contrast to Mr. Smith's attempts being stopped early in the network game, David P. Bloom deceived "100 clients into handing him over $10 million to invest in the Stock Market" before he too was caught. The *New York Times* writes that the 23-year-old Duke University graduate was able to sell bogus investment services to sophisticated New Yorkers by promising "prospective clients that his network would help them." His network was supposed to be made of wealthy, powerful connections. "But his network does not seem to have existed." It was only when people began talking to others in their own networks that they discovered the network was not "real" (Scardino, 1988, p. 8. Copyright © 1988 by The New York Times Company. Reprinted by permission).

tightly or loosely coupled (Weick, 1979). From a network perspective, communication is an interactive process, shaped by multiple strands of activities. The creation and interpretation of messages is built upon the associations, affiliations, and allegiances that bind individuals together.

The network metaphor views an organization as an open system of participants. People, groups, and other organizations are joined together by a variety of communicative relationships. Communication constitutes organizations; it is the essence of organized activity. Throughout this book, *organizations* are conceptualized as *identifiable social systems of interacting individuals pursuing multiple objectives through coordinated acts and relationships.* Not all people are joined directly; indirect linkages may be as important or even more important than direct links; not all relevant links are situated within the organizational boundaries; and not all linkages are equally significant. Further, people are often joined through multiple relationships in multiple contexts. *Communication,* always a joint occurrence, is the *mutual process of interpreting messages and creating understandings* (although not necessarily mutual understanding). *Organizational communication is the collective interactive process of generating and interpreting messages.* Networks of understandings are created through coordinated acts and relationships.

The organization consists of overlapping networks of interconnected individuals linked by patterned flows of information, services, influence, affect, and interpretations. Some networks are *formally prescribed,* bounded communication structures authorized by organizational charts. These structures may be explicitly defined, as in such cases as quality circles, project management teams, and departmental units. Positions in these networks are derived from the organization, expectations for role relations are part of a greater set of institutional norms, and specific individuals are interchangeable in a given position. The interaction of two people, whether a professor and a student or an engineer and the human resource manager, is determined by the characteristics of the organization, not, to any great extent, by the people themselves.

But these "relatively stable and enduring" positional networks (Monge & Eisenberg, 1987, p. 305) reflect only a limited sampling of organizational activities. "A prescribed organizational network provides pegs from which emergent networks hang" (Tichy, 1981, p. 227). Unplanned structures and unique communication patterns emerge for several reasons. First, organizations

---

## MAKING CONNECTIONS

*Henri Fayol* was a French manager who was one of the first practitioners to contribute to organizational theory. He began as an engineer in a large French mining company and 19 years later became the managing director. When Fayol took over, the company was on the verge of bankruptcy. During the 47 years Fayol ran the company, it flourished. Fayol presented his theory of management in a book titled *General and Industrial Management* (1925). Embedded within Fayol's 14 principles of management is a carefully prescribed organizational structure.

1. Division of work into specialized functions is the natural order.
2. Responsibility arises from authority, which is the right to give orders. Power exacts obedience.
3. Discipline arises from respect and fairness between workers and management.
4. Unity of command means that employees receive orders from only one supervisor.
5. Unity of direction indicates that there should be one plan for a group of activities having the same objective.
6. Individual interest should be subordinated to the general interest.
7. Remuneration of personnel should be fair but not overly generous.
8. Centralization (anything that reduces subordinates' importance in decision making) and decentralization (processes that increase subordinates' role in decision making) should be dependent upon the organization's circumstance.
9. A scalar chain (the linear system of hierarchical authority that stretches from the top to the bottom of the organization) may occasionally be modified through the use of a "bridge" or "gangplank" to join each link in the chain.
10. Order indicates that everyone and everything has a specific place in the organization.
11. Equity is preferred over justice. Justice is the execution of established conventions or rules without exception. Equity is kindness plus justice. Equity recognizes circumstances in which conventions don't apply.
12. Stability in tenure captures the idea that, because it takes a very long time to train people well, employees must be given a long time in their positions.
13. Exercise of initiative, to think out and ensure the success of a plan, is an important activity.
14. Esprit de corps indicates that personnel must not be divided and management should promote harmony among employees.

are so complex that formal designs can never anticipate all con-tingencies. Second, formal networks are rational systems, based on a finite number of potential linkages. The formal structure does not account for those connections individuals bring into the system that transcend either organizational boundaries and/or rationality. Third, individuals do not always conform to the inter-action sequences dictated by their organizational roles. Their own needs, emotions, self-interest, prior experiences, and indi-vidual perspectives penetrate organizational positions. In other words, *emergent networks* evolve because the limits imposed by the formal structures only constrain individual action, they do not control it. There are choices, although they may be from a set of socially constricted alternatives.

---

### MAKING CONNECTIONS

In 1982 seven people in Chicago, Illinois died in circumstances that baffled doctors. A 12-year-old, Mary Kellerman, from Elk Grove Village seemed to have died of a stroke; a 27-year-old man, Adam Janus from Arlington Heights, appeared to have suffered a massive heart attack; two victims came into emergency rooms with dilated pupils and low blood pressure, the rest died in their homes. With remarkable speed, investiga-tors were able to link all these deaths to Tylenol products that had been tampered with. How did this happen? Was it the formal, rational organiza-tional structure that allowed the officials to do their jobs so effectively?

*Newsweek* magazine's recounting of the events surrounding the discov-ery of the Tylenol tampering highlights the fluid boundaries of organiza-tional life and points to the importance of a "network" approach to under-standing organizational communication.

"Distraught over her daughter's death, Jeannita Kellerman heard about the mysterious Janus deaths and called Arlington Heights firefighter, Philip Cappitelli, the son-in-law of a friend, wondering if he knew any details. Cappitelli called his friend Richard Keyworth, a firefighter in Elk Grove Village. Though Keyworth was on vacation, he had gone into the Elk Grove fire house to collect his mail and remembered hearing from paramedics there that Mary Kellerman had taken an Extra Strength Tylenol capsule before collapsing. 'This is a wild stab, maybe it's the Tylenol,' Keyworth told Cappitelli. Cappitelli then checked with Arlington Heights paramedics and learned that the Janus family had taken Extra Strength Tylenol as well. Within hours, Arlington Heights and Elk Grove Village police had retrieved two bottles from both homes. Both bore the manu-facturer's lot number MC2880" ("The Tylenol Scare," 1982, p. 33. From *Newsweek*, Oct. 11, 1982, Newsweek, Inc. All rights reserved. Reprinted by permission).

The network metaphor incorporates the fundamental belief that organizational phenomena cannot be adequately understood by focusing on individual phenomena. Action must be considered insofar as it is embedded within larger sets of activities. Communication is collaborative and interdependent; there is no sharp dividing line between senders and receivers. Each relationship, and hence each communicative act, is essentially connected with the rest of the network (through direct and indirect links) and it is in that context that it must be understood. Therefore, instead of analyzing communication phenomena by dividing them into variables such as sender, receiver, or channel, emergent patterns become the primary focus of our inquiry. Each organization comprises multiple overlapping networks that can be distinguished on the basis of the analytic boundaries and specific criteria used to define a link.

## CONCEPTUALIZING
## NETWORK BOUNDARIES

Typically, *network boundaries* and the potential links are recognized on the basis of context. These might include all wage earners in a multinational organization, participants in a particular work group, the directors of the largest corporations in the United States, or members of a union. Implicit in this approach is the assumption that all relevant linkages can be found in some predetermined, formalized, or material, context.

*Organizational boundaries are never fixed.*

Throughout this text, we proceed from a very different assumption. *Network boundaries are always permeable and never stable.* Boundaries are diffuse and fluid because social action cannot be isolated; communication is at the intersection of contexts, actors, relations, and activities that cannot be disassociated from one another. Personal networks are continually contracting and expanding, thus organizational boundaries are never fixed.

ORGANIZATIONS AS
ELABORATED PERSONAL NETWORKS

Networks can be described at four interdependent levels of analysis: *personal, group, organizational,* and *interorganizational.* There will be a great deal of overlap as we move among these levels. The linkages that constitute personal networks are the threads of organizational networks. The patterns we observe at one level shape configurations at the next level. The crosscutting memberships of organizational members in multiple social circles weave together the social system. At every level, networks are dynamic, they are always changing, and the significant links are in flux while at the same time remaining somewhat stable across time and situations.

Our analysis begins at the individual level. *Personal or ego-centered networks* comprise all the linkages an individual has across social spheres. The nature, intimacy, and impact of these

---

### MAKING CONNECTIONS

When first considered, the diffuse nature of network boundaries and thereby the potential size of networks may seem overwhelming. But the world is far more interconnected and small than we have imagined. Most of us have had the experience of meeting a brand-new colleague and finding out we have a good friend or relative in common. It is not that unusual for a lighthearted conversation with a complete stranger in an elevator in a large city to yield the information that the other person is the brother of a friend of yours from college some 3,000 miles away. These serendipitous connections seem amazing in a world of almost 5 billion people.

But the expression "it's a small world" means more than a ride at Disneyland or an interesting anecdote. Research by Stanley Milgram and associates (1967) demonstrated that, from a network perspective, it is, indeed, a small world. Milgram asked people to advance a message to an unknown person (target) through any acquaintance who was more likely than him- or herself to know the target person. His results showed that it took on average 5.5 steps for a randomly selected person in Nebraska to reach a randomly selected person in Massachusetts. This "small world" phenomenon has been replicated in several studies across cultures, contexts, and continents (Shotland, 1976) and has even become part of a national advertising campaign for a multinational telecommunication company.

relationships change over time. At different stages of our lives, at varying points in our careers, specific linkages will have a greater or lesser influence on how we think, feel, and behave on and off the job. For example, as young children, our aunts and uncles may be central to the core of "significant others" within our network, but over time they usually move to the periphery. Nonetheless, although we may not think of them as having relevant connections to our adult work lives, these adult attitudes and values are the original sources of information about what a job is, what types of jobs are available, what it means to work, and how one communicates at work. Lively dinner table discussions about Aunt Ethel, for example, a metallurgist, who was able to travel around the world, opens vistas and possible avenues to pursue that would not have even been considered without such conversations.

The traditional model of career choice suggests that individuals come to career decisions after rational, systematic searches for information (Soelberg, 1967). More recent models of "anticipatory socialization" (Jablin, 1987) and the critical contact theory of job choice (Feldman, 1988) recognize that our individual networks—family, teachers, peers, friends, our friends' friends, and so on—greatly influence our conception of what work means, our knowledge about specific types of work, and our actions on the job. Friends and job incumbents tend to have higher credibility about jobs than recruiters or professors (Fisher, Ilgen, & Troyer, 1979); even fishing buddies, bridge partners, and relatives may strongly influence our attitudes about politics at work. For example, a refusal to cross a picket line may have little to do with communication at work; a favorite uncle may have been a union steward for 40 years and the personal costs of going against the union may far outweigh the professional benefits found in management's anti-union arguments. Decisions about job transfers, promotions, and international relocations have all been found to be strongly influenced by the direct and indirect links in our personal networks (Adler, 1991).

Networks at the group, organizational, and interorganizational levels are the interwoven composites of personal networks. Although seemingly discrete, these levels are actually

# MAKING CONNECTIONS

In today's global economy, there is an increasing need to send employees overseas. Except in the most exceptional cases, each relocation directly and indirectly involves several others in the employees' personal networks. These include co-workers staying at the home base, family members and friends remaining at home (perhaps elderly parents, children in college), and family members joining the employee at the new work site.

Whereas in 1973 only 10% of executives who were offered foreign assignments declined the offers, in 1987 over 40% refused (Driessnack, 1987). Despite millions of dollars spent on intercultural and language skill training, between 16%-40% of expatriate managers do not assimilate successfully. Over 20% of expatriate managers request to return home before the assignment is completed. According to Organization Resources Counseling, Inc., there is a more than 40% attrition rate for those employees who have had no adaptability screening or cultural training, and 25% for those who have had some training. And productivity rates of expatriate managers are often much lower than expected prior to relocation. Overall, American companies lose approximately $2 billion per year in direct costs associated with failed foreign overseas assignments (Berge, 1987).

Why is there such a dismal record of expatriate success? Several researchers suggest that the high rate of refusal even to go overseas and the lack of success of those who go abroad are closely associated with the tenacity of multinational corporations to hold on to the myopic "myth of separate worlds." The empirical data indicate that *spousal involvement* in the decision to relocate as well as the spouse's *positive adjustment to the foreign country* is critical to the expatriate employee's successful assimilation and work performance (Thornburg, 1990). Yet multinational corporations, for the most part, have not considered the spouse to be an important part of the foreign assignment.

For example, multinational corporations have failed to recognize the significant contribution of the spouse's income. Loss of the second income dramatically increases the family's stress. Of employees who relocate, 47% have working spouses. In a study conducted by Allied Van Lines, Inc., 84% of the 241 corporate executives who responded to a survey said their spouses were not offered any type of job assistance (Thornburg, 1990).

Further, joint career decision making has become more common in American culture. Spousal connections to church, family, volunteer organizations, and professional obligations are no longer relegated to secondary concerns, and spouses are not convinced of the relative advantage of uprooting. Professional employees tend to have professional spouses who are not willing or expected to sacrifice their own careers for their spouses' potential advancement (Black & Stephens, 1989).

Most companies do not even offer language classes for the family although it is the spouse, not the expatriate employee, who communicates more frequently with locals when first arriving in the new country. It is the spouse's responsibility to settle the family into an everyday routine as well as to offer support by hosting business dinner parties and accompanying the employee to work-related social functions.

alternative ways of arranging the same data. At the *group level*, individuals are clustered together who (at a given point in time) are more intensely connected to one another than they are to others in the organization. Each person, however, still maintains a set of unique linkages that transcend the group's identity yet strongly influence group activity.

Traditionally, when we consider groups in organizations we think of a "collection of 3 or more organizational members who interact (more or less regularly) over time, are psychologically cognizant of one another, perceive themselves as a group and most important are embedded within a network of interlocking tasks, roles and expectations" (Jablin & Sussman, 1983, p. 26). The collective perception of unity often assumes definite boundaries and locates people in relation to those boundaries (in- and out-groups). The internal dynamics of the group are imagined to be self-contained; if there is conflict, solutions are sought within the narrow range of communication that takes place within the group; ineffectual decision making is associated with dysfunctional intragroup communication (e.g., not all alternatives were

---

### MAKING CONNECTIONS

Ironically, the most obvious place where a self-contained view of organizational groups and thus organizational communication can be found is in the early network research (Bavelas, 1950; Leavitt, 1951). Networks were conceived as the number and arrangement of communication channels among group members. These researchers assumed that the optimum pattern of communication was derived from requirements of the task independent from anything else. The group was the container within which communication across different types of channel configurations took place.

Overall, the researchers found that wheel, chain, and Y—that is, the centralized networks—were most efficient for simple problem solving and routine matters. The less centralized circle was least efficient in terms of time but made fewer mistakes. When multiple operations had to be performed and adaptation and innovation were required, decentralized networks were most effective. Members of decentralized networks reported greater satisfaction with the group; isolates were less satisfied and less productive (Shaw, 1954). Being in a key network position served to elevate a person into a leadership position but also led to the individual experiencing information overload (Leavitt, 1951).

considered, criteria were not developed); and group climate is separated and isolated from the larger context.

The container metaphor does not let us see how *bona fide groups* actually work because it ignores two major features of groups: (a) *stable yet permeable boundaries* and (b) *interdependence with context* (Putnam & Stohl, 1990). The permeability of boundaries refers to

---

## MAKING CONNECTIONS

A *bona fide group perspective* counters the prevailing notion that groups can be understood in isolation from their environments. For example, organizational leaders often believe that groups will make the best decisions if they set aside external affiliations and make rational, "non-political" judgments. But, as the selection below indicates, groups may fail at their tasks precisely because they intentionally ignore a group's permeable boundaries and its overlapping memberships.

"A college dean appointed key opinion leaders from various committees to a blue-ribbon committee charged with revising the school's core curriculum requirements. The committee's proposal was to be submitted to the faculty senate for ratification. Since core curriculum proposals were notoriously 'hot potatoes', members of the committee realized that input from the faculty, students, and other administrators was vital to the success of the proposal. Hence they viewed their roles as linking pins to external groups, but not as representatives of any particular constituencies.

"The Dean admonished members of the committee to disavow departmental identities, to transform petty differences, and to make a decision based on quality undergraduate education. In effect, they were asked to relinquish their external affiliations in making group decisions. Although members sought input from various constituencies, investigated models at other institutions, and developed a proposal that transcended intergroup differences, the diverse and often antithetical positions of their constituencies were never fully ironed out in the final proposal. Indeed, the one member who consistently functioned as a representative of his external group's position became a deviant within the group because he did not follow the committee in relinquishing 'petty' departmental biases.

"At the end of the deliberations, committee members tried to sell the final proposal to their colleagues. After a heated debate and split vote on the faculty senate, the proposal was rejected in a faculty wide referendum. Ironically, the committee's deliberations would suggest that it was a model of rational decision making. Members were vigilant in pursuing their goal of a workable, high-quality set of core requirements for undergraduates. Issues were confronted, conflict was open, and multiple alternatives were presented and tested. The group failure stemmed, in part, from a norm of disavowing implicit representatives on a task whose ultimate success hinged on integrating widely diffused positions outside the group" (Putnam & Stohl, 1990, p. 259).

the fluid and dynamic nature of group membership. The context refers to the ways that groups depend upon and contribute to their environment.

Consider the communication in any of the several groups of which you are a part (student government, racquetball club, the honors program). The communication inside the group is strongly influenced by members' personal networks (e.g., Are some of the members related to one another? Do members have other friends in common?) and by the degree to which they are tightly or loosely interlocked with other subunits both within and outside the formal organization (e.g., Are the officers all members of the same sorority or fraternity? Are group members involved in many other university activities?). Researchers find that high-performing teams tend to be more highly linked with other groups in the organization than less effective groups (Tushman & Scanlan, 1981). Gladstein-Ancona and Caldwell (1987) interviewed product team managers and members and found that the network roles associated with effective product development teams were boundary spanning roles: scouts and sentries, who deal with information that comes into the team, and guards and ambassadors, who influence how others perceive the team. There may even be a communicative trade-off between internal and external group effectiveness. In several organizational studies, the most effective teams, as judged by external judges, were ones who had frequent contacts with the outside environment. Alternatively, the most cohesive and highly satisfied groups interacted infrequently with outside constituents (e.g., Ancona & Caldwell, 1988).

The network view of organizations also highlights the probability of future interaction in other contexts moderating group process even when the two situations are unrelated. The knowledge that there will be continued interactions in the future is likely to reinforce attachment and cooperation in the present. Heide (1992) attributes this effect to what he calls "the shadow of the future." He argues that the knowledge that a relationship may be long lasting influences actors to cooperate in the present so that they will not adversely affect interactions in the future.

Most significant, the critical and essential links for understanding the group may be outside the organization itself. Multiple group memberships are the building blocks of organizations. Our diverse set of linkages integrate the system but our
"partial inclusion" may also result in divided loyalties and less-
ening commitment (Putnam, 1989).

The *organizational network* transcends individual relationships
and directs primary attention to the implications of emergent
structures. Communicative, cognitive, and affective processes
are embedded in a larger social context. For example, in a study
of how involvement in communication networks affects workers'
commitment to an organization, Eisenberg, Monge, and Miller
(1983) found there was no simple relationship between one's
position in organizational networks and attitudes toward the
organization. Highly connected employees who were not involved in their jobs were more committed to their jobs than those
who had low job involvement and were not enmeshed within the
system's work-related network. Being highly connected in the
network, however, did not foster commitment when employees
were already involved in their jobs.

Organizational networks are also the primary contextual de-
terminants of conflict activity (Putnam & Poole, 1987). Role conflict is often the direct result of membership in multiple networks;
conflict styles are chosen, in part, on the basis of the two conflictual parties' positions in the formal network (Putnam & Wilson,
1982); and incompatible goals arise in the sense-making activities
of various networks. Complex organizational structures exacerbate conflict. According to Putnam and Poole (1987): "When
complexity increases, communication networks fragment and
lead to different perspectives within units. If this condition is
combined with high interdependence, conflict between units
increases" (p. 575).

At the *interorganizational level,* personal linkages are depersonalized insofar as they link one organization to another but reper-
sonalized in that they still retain their interpersonal qualities.
Interorganizational linkages usually reflect the resource needs
and surplus of a system (Van de Ven, Emmett, & Koenig, 1980)

while the personal nature of the ties generates trust and discour-
ages betrayal of one another (Granovetter, 1985). The interpersonal ties among boundary spanners (i.e., those individuals who
link organizations with one another) play such a major role in the
maintenance of interorganizational relationships that many corporations find it necessary to resort to contractual practices and
legal sanctions to protect the interests of the organization rather
than the individuals (Macaulay, 1963). Seabright, Leventhal, and
Fichman (1992) found that, although changes in an organization's needs (in this case, a client of an auditing firm) increased
the likelihood of switching auditors, the personal attachments of
individuals primarily responsible for the interorganizational
linkages (in this specific case, the company's financial officers)

---

### MAKING CONNECTIONS

One of the distinguishing characteristics of the Japanese economy is the
close linkage between government, industry, and education. Interorganizational linkages are so important to Japanese management that enormous
amounts of time are dedicated to pursuing and cementing these connections. For example, government officials of MITI, the Ministry of International Trade and Industry, which is responsible for implementing Japan's
industrial policy, frequently meet with the company managers of Japan's
largest firms and industries to discuss business needs and government
goals and to establish relationships. Business and government are seen as
partners rather than adversaries in industrial development (Mitroff, 1987).

But networks of cooperation in Japan go even further than the links
between corporations and government. Networks of firms, called *keiretsu*,
are formed around large industries such as steel (Sumitomo Shoji), chemical production (Mitsui Bussan), and textiles (C. Itoh). These *keiretsu* distinguish Tokyo-style capitalism from Western capitalism.

Mitsubishi is Japan's largest *keiretsu*. This interlinked group includes
several companies that share the Mitsubishi name (Mitsubishi Heavy
Industries, Mitsubishi Electric, Mitsubishi Motors, Nikon Corporation,
and the Kirin Brewery). The network is monolithic and exclusive; they
trade, buy parts, and enter ventures only with members of the *keiretsu* (Dun
& Bradstreet, 1992). Historical bonds among these companies run deep but
the relationships are not taken for granted. The chairmen and presidents
of the Mitsubishi companies have weekly lunches intended to provide a
comfortable environment for interaction. Although they discuss national
and international political events and talk about the direction of the group,
the main goal of these lunches is to create and sustain the personal relationships that are essential for doing any type of business in Japan (Sanger,
1992).

decreased the likelihood of switching firms. In other words, the personal nature of the ties precluded the organization from necessarily acting in its own best interests.

Interorganizational networks represent powerful connections: at one extreme are monopolies that connive to deprive free competition; at the other end, strong interorganizational ties help legitimize less established organizations. The United Way is an interorganizational network that exhibits both these aspects. It links several community agencies together that otherwise would not be able to raise large amounts of money and hence helps these organizations meet their commitments and thrive. On the other hand, United Way strongly controls which social agencies and services are able to survive. Organizational boards that do not "work" well with the executives of United Way or do not share similar social visions may be strongly disadvantaged in the search for funding.

CONCEPTUALIZING NETWORK LINKS

Networks, neither observable nor tangible, are symbolic representations of connectedness. The fundamental unit of any network is the link. Depending upon how we define *link*, the membership and configuration of networks change and our understanding of organizing processes is somewhat altered. Broadly construed, a network link represents the presence of a connection, a relationship between two people.

Typically, network links are distinguished on the basis of whether or not a particular type of interactive exchange takes place among participants in some predetermined social system. For example, we can determine who interacts to obtain expressive (affective network), instrumental (power network), cognitive (informative network), or objective (goods and services network) resources. If a person only communicates with another about job information, she would be linked in a cognitive network but not in an affective network. We can specify these networks even further and identify the predominant content of messages among dyadic linkages, including whether or not people talk about production, innovation, maintenance (Albrecht & Ropp, 1984; Farace, Monge, & Russell, 1977), or the type of

functional challenge—that is, technical, political, or cultural—
that is addressed by the discourse (Tichy, 1981). Danowski (1980)
found that the relationships between network structures and
employee attitudes and beliefs systematically varied depending
upon which type of network was examined. Group connectivity
and attitude belief uniformity, for example, were closely associated in production and innovation networks but not in maintenance networks.

Network links may also be distinguished on the basis of the
patterns of functional relationships people have with one another. Guetzkow (1965) identified five types of organizational
networks: authority, friendship, expert, status, and information
exchange. Each network was associated with particular message
functions.

Network memberships overlap and the degree to which the
patterns are entwined exerts a strong influence on organizing
processes and organizational environments. Folger and Poole
(1984) identify four dominant themes of organizational experience that serve as the foundation for *organizational climate: dominance and authority relations, degree of supportiveness, sense of group
identity,* and *interdependence.* Network patterns contribute to each
of these themes. For example, when a leader is a central figure in
the authority and friendship networks across the organization
and most friendship links are intraorganizational, there is likely
to be a highly developed sense of supportiveness and group
identity as well as more egalitarian authority relations. When
network structures are discrete, do not overlap, and relationships
are unidimensional, individuals are more likely to experience a
higher degree of dependence (as compared with interdependence) and identify with smaller subunits. Furthermore, perceptions of communication climate vary systematically with an individual's position in the networks. Studies have found that
people who were more fully integrated into organizational networks perceived the climate more positively (Albrecht, 1979;
Reynolds & Johnson, 1982). In other words, the configuration and
overlap of networks influence climate by directly influencing the
four themes.

Although the above discussion may seem to suggest that networks have discrete functions, this is not the case. Messages are
multifunctional (e.g., the message

"please come here" may serve as a
request and a sign of affection) and
hence the networks in which these
messages are enacted serve multiple

> *Network links serve
> multiple functions.*

functions. Friendship networks, for example, are not merely sets
of linked friends who like to go jogging everyday at noon; messages may cover the full array of organizational experience including decision premises, resource mobilization, and information transfer. Organizational friendship networks often mirror
and replicate the structures of task-related networks (Lincoln &
Miller, 1979). It is not surprising therefore that when women and
minorities do not have access to the friendships networks of the
majority they are also denied access to a great deal of job-related
information. These exclusionary practices are rarely explicit and
often happen without malice or forethought. Intentional or not,
however, they serve to maintain the powerful positions of the
dominant group.

Links may also be determined on the basis of "sharedness."
Semantic networks, for example, are derived from an analysis of
the extent to which individuals' meanings and interpretations of
messages overlap. The organizational picture drawn from these
linkages gives us a sense of its cultural texture. Monge and
Eisenberg (1987) suggest that "convergence on interpretations is
one indication of cultural diversity or homogeneity, and cliques
resulting from such an analysis may even provide evidence of
subcultures" (p. 333). Note that, in semantic networks, people
may be linked together who never communicate directly with
one another—they may not even know one another—but what
links them together is the similarity of interpretations.

Links can also be distinguished by their location within larger
network configurations. Rogers and Agarwala-Rogers (1976) identified several organizational network roles that provide useful
descriptions of a link's position within the organization. *Gatekeep-
ers* control messages flowing from one segment to another; *liai-*

*sons* connect two or more cliques in the system without belonging
to any clique; *linking pins* or *bridges* are members of two or more

## MAKING CONNECTIONS

In 1988 the U.S. Supreme Court upheld a New York State law prohibit-
ing men-only policies at clubs that (a) had over 400 members, (b) served
meals regularly, and (c) had members who conducted business at the site.
Since that time women have become members of groups such as the Rotary
Club, the Lions Club, the Friar's Club, and Kiwanis International. In
joining these clubs, women gained legal access to the social meeting places
where civic, political, and corporate leaders carry out a great deal of
business, share information, and develop future partnerships.

Women, however, are still denied entry to the inner circle of power both
formally and informally. Many elite private organizations refuse to admit
women and communities that do not have local statutes barring discrimination against women do not have to comply with the Supreme Court
action.

Furthermore, the informal segregation of men's and women's social networks continues to minimize women's access to power. Cynthia Cockburn,
a British sociologist, in her book *In the Way of Women: Men's Resistance to
Sex Equality in Organizations* (1991), starkly illustrates the ways in which
gender dynamics, embedded in the social networks of organizations,
disadvantage women. In one narrative, she describes how "male managers and office workers had over many decades generated a male social
world both within and outside work from which women were *excluded*"
[emphasis in original]. Notice, in the excerpt below, how the men's words
marginalize and separate women, not allowing them to become enmeshed
in what is clearly an important organizational system.

"Men (especially men of similar grade within a department or team)
would frequently drink and socialize together at the end of the day and
over the weekend. Women told me they felt their absence from these all
male gatherings impeded their progress, cutting them out from important
sources of information. 'There's a lot of "in" things I don't get to find out,'
said one young [female] manager. And indeed, the men affirmed the value
of their socializing. 'We have a phrase: you'll learn more in the pub than
you will in the store.' Some men clearly felt women were incapable of
relating, even to each other, in the same social way as men were wont to
do. 'I just don't envisage that—they are just—they operate on a different
level altogether' said an older man. 'It's a level that obviously appeals to
*them* [emphasis in original]. But I don't see them as having the same
informal camaraderie, if you like'. The socializing among the predomi-
nantly white male workforce may sometimes exclude black men. Yet black
men too can value the male bonding process. Thus a young black junior
manager said that for him socializing with male colleagues was the important thing. 'I'm not being anti-women,' he said, 'I suppose ladies may feel
they've got things *they* want to talk about' " (p. 152).

overlapping groups; and *isolates* have a low degree of connectedness anywhere in the system. Isolates tend to be less satisfied,
liaisons more influential, and linking pins often have greater job
satisfaction than isolates.

This approach is somewhat limited insofar as the boundaries
are preset and the potential pools of network members are determined a priori. From the perspective of this book, we are all
*boundary spanners.* Network roles such as *scout, ambassador, sentry,*
and *guard* capture the ways in which the permeability of group
interaction is enacted (Ancona & Caldwell, 1988). We are all
members of multiple groups and bring those affiliations with us
into the workplace; we translate and interpret equivocal information in large part based upon our external linkages and we move
into and influence one another through an endless series of
textured links.

In summary, a network link always represents a relationship
between people although the nature of the connection varies
considerably. Links may represent any type of communication
contact or symbolize shared interpretations that do not necessarily reflect actual communication activity. Not all links are equal.
They can vary along several dimensions including orientation,
reciprocity, strength, symmetry, and multiplexity. Each of these
qualities affects organizational communication processes and
will be discussed in the chapter on relationships. But first we
must explore several structural dimensions of networks. It is
these patterns, derived from relations among participants, that
shape organizational experience.

## NETWORK DIMENSIONS

*Size.* Organizations and networks come in all sizes. Small en-
trepreneurial firms may have as few as two or three employees;
large multinational corporations may employ over 200,000 people. Depending upon how we define a link, personal networks
may also range from two to thousands. If we just consider a
network of acquaintances, for example (people you could recognize and call by name if you met them), size ranges from 500 to

2,000, with the average individual having at least 1,000 acquaintances (Rogers & Kincaid, 1981).

Although there is some literature that indicates that people with very small networks tend to be the least productive and least satisfied members of the system (Roberts & O'Reilly, 1979), have fewer support buffers (Caplan, 1976), and are less likely to feel integrated into a group (Stohl, 1989b), most organizational scholars realize that size is important in terms of its relation to other network attributes rather than as an independent causal factor. Network size is dependent upon where and how we draw network boundaries. Moreover, individuals may have small organizational networks for several reasons. Some jobs demand isolation. Some people are more solitary by nature and they would be extraordinarily unhappy if they were in a job that demanded them to be outgoing and gregarious. Additionally, individuals may be enmeshed in so many networks that are large and demanding, they may prefer a job whose defining characteristics are that they work quietly and alone. Other network demands may preclude the establishment of large task-related networks. A worker with five children, for example, does not have the same time available as does a single person to become involved in social networks at work.

*Interconnectedness.* Interconnectedness or density is the *ratio of actual to potential contacts* in the network. "It is the proportion of linkages that exist relative to the total number of contacts that would exist if everyone were linked directly to everyone else" (Monge & Eisenberg, 1987, p. 317). There have been dozens of studies across several disciplines that indicate the far-reaching systematic effect density has on an individual's attitudes, daily behavior, and communication (e.g., Bott, 1957; Milroy & Margrain, 1980; Stohl, 1989a).

*Highly interconnected networks tend to be composed of strong, close ties.*

Highly interconnected networks tend to be composed of strong, close ties. Diversity is minimized in these networks. Sororities and fraternities are usually highly interconnected groups. Families and other types of organizations tend to vary in the degree of interconnectedness. Your family may be comprised of closely knit relatives, adults' friends, children's friends, teachers, and co-workers, most of whom know and communicate with one another. Other families may have segmented, low-density networks. Family members do not know one another's friends, children's relationships are not integrated into the family system, and work connections constitute a separate and independent sphere of experience.

Highly interconnected networks tend to have several dynamics in common: (a) norms and expectations are agreed upon and made apparent; (b) there are multiple and consistent models of "appropriate behavior" and interpretations; (c) people are rewarded for normative action. Thus there is a greater degree of pressure for people to adopt the norms and values (including

---

### MAKING CONNECTIONS

There has been much empirical work that supports a theory of the *"strength of weak ties."* Weak ties are links that are loosely connected to the rest of the network and therefore less likely to be socially involved with one another and more likely to be connected to some other set of ties not otherwise represented in a person's network. Strong ties are highly interconnected, overlapping in contact and content. Information from a strong tie is likely to replicate the information already available in the network. Thus a person with few weak ties will be deprived of information from distant parts of the social system and will be confined to provincial news and views of their close friends.

*Mark Granovetter* (1974), a sociologist who originally developed the theory of "the strength of weak ties," writes: "This deprivation [not having weak ties] will not only insulate them from the latest ideas and fashions, but may put them in a disadvantaged position in the labor market, where advancement can depend on knowing about appropriate job openings at just the right time" (p. 72). Granovetter's (1974) classic study of recent job changers found that professional, technical, and managerial workers were more likely to hear about jobs through weak ties (27.8%) than through strong ties (16.7%).

The deprivation of new ideas and information adds to the normative pressures that are embedded in a highly interconnected network of strong ties. Research with widows, for example, found that short-term adaptation was associated with dense, interconnected networks, whereas adaptation over the long term was associated with loosely connected networks with

*(continued)*

linguistic and non-verbal norms) of the local group when en-meshed in a high-density rather than a low-density network.

In many ways a highly interconnected network is similar to what Deal and Kennedy (1982) call a strong culture. A strong culture represents a system of informal rules that detail explicitly what are appropriate and inappropriate ways to behave. Deal and Kennedy describe the cultural network as the carrier of the corporate values and heroic mythology. The roles in this "cul-tural" network—spies, storyteller, priests, whisperers, cabals—form a hidden hierarchy and interpret the significance of infor-mation to employees—tell how things should be taken.

*Centrality.* Centrality is also an important network attribute and can refer to an individual as well as to the entire network. The concentration of power, decision making, and control over resources in one segment of the organization usually is consid-

---

several weak ties. Strong ties did not give the woman room for experimen-tation and change but did provide nurturance. People in these networks often talked to each other and so were able to make sure the widow was not alone and was provided a great deal of emotional support, but there was no room for her to try new things. They all had known her husband, all agreed on what was best for her, what he wanted, and so on. The messages she received therefore were all very consistent and redundant, reinforcing the same types of behaviors and patterns she had always been involved in. Women with weak ties, however, were given more opportu-nity for risk and change; they received a diversity of advice and informa-tion and so were able to make new lives for themselves more easily (Hirsch, 1979).

In a study of family networks, Elizabeth Bott (1957) found that, when the husband's and wife's acquaintance networks were highly intercon-nected, conjugal roles tended to be segregated and stereotypically sex typed. When the networks were not connected, conjugal roles tended to be joint and less stereotypically divided. In other words, the more intercon-nected the network, the greater adherence to traditional societal norms.

Linguistic pressures in dense networks have also been found to repli-cate norm-enforcing functions. Milroy and Margrain (1980) found that teenagers from three distinct Belfast inner cities were differentially pres-sured to speak in the local style depending on network density. The greater the network density, the more loyalty shown to the particular vernacular language of the local group and the less adherence to the larger societal communication standards.

ered to be evidence that a system is centralized. Highly centralized networks are associated with mechanistic systems (Weick, 1987). Highly *centralized* systems tend to have a high degree of *vertical differentiation, low levels of horizontal differentiation, many isolates,* and *few liaisons* (Pearce & David, 1983). These attributes tend to have a negative impact on performance in a volatile environment. *Decentralized* systems, associated with more organic systems, are apparent when there is *more participation* by many in the decision-making process, when *information is more widely shared,* and when there is a *greater degree of communication* within, across, and between subsystems. The high connectedness associated with organic decentralized networks, as well as the high level of horizontal differentiation, are associated with high performance in volatile environments (Pearce & David, 1983).

## ❑ Final Connections

The network metaphor helps us see each individual as an environmental resource or boundary spanner bringing with him or her a unique set of affiliations that influence the groups of which he or she is a part. Furthermore, each group member represents his or her "otherness" to the organization. Recognizing that groups do not operate in isolation from their environment, that attitudes, perceptions, and communication are the composite result of embeddedness within overlapping networks, gives us tools to address organizational problems such as tokenism and discrimination. By bridging the private and the personal, we can see that organizational communication is not a linear process. *Network boundaries are stable yet permeable, network memberships foster individuality,* and *networks stimulate and constrain innovation.* To understand organizational communication, we must look at the linkages across social, political, and economic domains and recognize these are not discrete arenas of social action.

# PART II

# The Complex Matrix

# 3

# *Messages*

*The first two chapters emphasized the importance of networks for understanding organizational experience. In this chapter, we focus on messages, what people say, write, and interpret us meaningful. Whether verbal or non-verbal, intentional or unintentional, messages are the foundation upon which the meanings of organizational experience are built.*

Messages are fundamental to communication. It is impossible to imagine any relationship or social system that could exist in the absence of messages. Couples, families, social groups, voluntary associations, business firms, international organizations are all tied together by people sharing messages. How people interpret messages varies, but the need to enact and make sense of our environment through creating and receiving messages is universal.

Each day thousands of messages are generated within organizational networks. Occasionally, we may send or receive truly "memorable messages," messages that stand out, hold great significance for one or many of the people in our network, and are precisely remembered over a long period of time. Nearly all of us can precisely recall at least one message that has had a major influence on our lives. These messages are usually given in private rather than public settings and are received from someone of higher stature than the recipient: a teacher to a student, a parent to a child, a coach to an athlete. Within the workplace, such messages are usually communicated by a person higher up in the hierarchy and help us interpret organizational events and expectations as well as providing guidelines for appropriate behavior. In one medium-sized company, for example, people remember being told, "There's plenty of time to sleep when you die" (i.e., you should never seem too overworked or tired to do any job), "Your first priority is commodities" (i.e., family concerns have no place in this company), and "Don't kick the king, unless you kill him" (i.e., politics is a deadly game in this organization, be prepared; Stohl, 1986a). Sometimes these messages become the cornerstone for an entire organization. For example, James Burke, the CEO of Johnson & Johnson, a company known for its innovative environment and substantial tolerance for failure, often repeats a message given to him by General Johnson (the founder of the company), "If I weren't making mistakes, I wasn't making decisions."

More often, however, specific messages are not that memorable. Because messages are both ubiquitous and fundamental to organizing, we usually pay little attention to their complexity. As in any system of relationships, messages often become the specific focus of interest only in the early stages of a relationship and/or when something has gone wrong. But messages are the primary means by which roles are clarified, social support is provided, power is realized, and coordination is made possible within an organization. Messages are, in short, fundamental to understanding our organizational experience. Thus messages are central in our definition of *organizational communication*—the collective interactive process of generating and interpreting *messages*.

Two of the most common complaints about organizations focus on messages: "We don't get adequate information. No one tells me anything. I'm left in the dark." and "There's too much information. I am overloaded, I can't do everything they tell me to do." Although these concerns seem to contradict one another, we often experience *message overload* and *message inadequacy* simultaneously. The messages we receive are not always the messages we need or want. Messages may complicate rather than simplify, confuse rather than clarify. Communication is not necessarily the answer to the problem; it may be the cause of the problem. Messages vary in content, interest, and importance; they come through different channels; they create different patterns of response and link networks in different ways. Even the same message may have different effects depending upon who issues the message, the timing of its reception, and the context in which it is said.

In this chapter, we examine the critical features of messages and consider how messages, relationships, and meaning are interdependent. We explore how our positions within organizational networks and our experiences outside the organization affect why we send and how we interpret messages.

There are four major points about messages that this chapter incorporates: (a) *messages operate at multiple levels*; (b) *messages have multiple meanings*; (c) *messages assume multiple forms* (e.g., verbal/non-verbal, formal/informal); and (d) *messages perform multiple functions*. First, however, we address the most fundamental issue of all, that is, what a message is.

## ❑ What Is a Message?

Coming home from work late in the evening, you see the kitchen light is on. You look up and smile—it's a message from your partner that he or she is up waiting for you, he or she loves you. Or you may cringe, the light means he or she is up and angry—you're too late. Or perhaps you don't interpret the light as a message at all, it doesn't mean anything, you assume someone just forgot to turn out the light. Is the light a message? It could be.

From a "receiver's" point of view, anything that triggers meaning is a message. So things like where you are seated, the type of furniture in your office, where you are assigned a parking spot, and the order in which you get to see the boss are potential messages, whether they are intentional or not. From a sender's point of view, we must remember that messages are not "things" that can be transferred directly from one person to another but are the stimulus for sense making.

Basically, there are two types of messages. *Ostensive messages* are the actual text (these can be verbal, non-verbal, paralinguistic cues, or artifacts). *Internally experienced messages* are the interpretations of these ostensive messages and represent the intentions of the sender and the interpretations of receiver(s) (Stohl & Redding, 1987).

Interpretations of messages are based upon experiences both within and outside the organizational context. The message, "We

---

### MAKING CONNECTIONS

In today's world of plant closings, downsizing, and corporate restructuring, many people try to read "messages" related to their future in their company. The efforts to derive meanings from data other than specific verbal messages, however, is not new to today's uncertain environment. In ambiguous situations, people have always tended to look beyond explicitly focused messages to make sense of their environment. This quest for meaning often results in interpretations that are rational, consistent, and yet completely inappropriate. Take, for example, an actual case presented in *Roethlisberger* and *Dickson*'s (1939) classic human relations text *Management and the Worker*. They describe a situation in which a departmental move created a set of "messages" that resulted in a serious misinterpretation of a situation.

Because new departmental space was smaller, management needed to shift seating arrangements and have four people sit across the aisle from the rest of the office pool. Three of the people who were given these desks were soon going to be transferred to other work, so management thought this would be the least disruptive arrangement. The decision of the fourth person was based solely upon social factors. They chose an older man who was well acquainted with the three women. In an interview with the authors, the male employee told the authors how he interpreted the move and the messages he received from management.

*(continued)*

need you to work late for the next week," will be interpreted differently depending one's personal situation. If a child is going off to college, the extra income may be welcomed; if the child is very young, the cost of baby-sitting may offset the gains from overtime; if the employee is newly in love, the necessity to cancel an evening on the town may be extremely costly. Furthermore, if the request is made by an individual who is perceived as untrustworthy by others in your work network, you may be concerned about staying after hours with him or her. If people within your network have already made several comments regarding this person's romantic intentions, you may think the request for overtime is a ruse, and act quite rudely. If you are the sender's boss, you may think the statement highly inappropriate. Or, if in your last job working late only meant an extra 15 minutes, you may not even perceive the message as being particularly important. In other words, a person's position, network affiliations,

---

"He felt that his supervisor evaluated him in the same way he evaluated the women. The women were being transferred to other types of work; consequently he felt he would be transferred before too long. Two of the women were being returned to jobs in the shop. He felt that he himself might be transferred to the shop; and there was nothing he dreaded more. Having dwelt on speculations like these for awhile, the employee recalled with alarm that his name had been omitted from the current issue of the house telephone directory. This omission had been accidental. The house directory, however, constitutes a sort of social register. Names of the shop people below the rank of assistant foreman were not printed unless they were employed in some special capacity requiring contacts with other organizations. With the exception of typists and certain clerical groups, the names of all office people were listed. The fact that his name had been omitted from the directory now took on new significance for the employee. It tended to reinforce his growing conviction that he was about to be transferred to a shop position. He became so preoccupied over what might happen to him that for a time he could scarcely work" (p. 214).

Roethlisberger and Dickson do not tell us what finally happened to this employee, but we can imagine the vicious cycle that might have ensued. One message after another was interpreted in such a manner as to convince the employee his work was considered below standard. These concerns would distract his attention from tasks and the employee's work would suffer. The manager would notice and, not understanding the reason for his poor performance, would consider transferring the employee—a self-fulfilling prophecy!

cultural identifications, and previous work experience may influence what a message "means." As Rogers and Kincaid (1981) state: *"The uniqueness of an individual's personal network is responsible for the uniqueness of his meanings"* (p. 45).

The different texture and composition of individuals' communication networks greatly affect the types of messages people

---

### MAKING CONNECTIONS

According to *Hall* and *Hall* (1989), differences in message production and interpretation are apparent when people from high- and low-context cultures interact in the workplace. They suggest that Japanese, Arabic, southern European, and other high-context cultures (HC) have extensive and elaborate information networks among family, friends, colleagues, and clients who are involved in close personal relationships. As a result, for most transactions within these cultures, business people do not require nor do they expect much more background; the context is already very rich with information in which to carry on the interaction. Low-context cultures (LC), including the United States, Germany, and other northern European groups, compartmentalize their personal relationships, their work, and many aspects of day-to-day life. Consequently, each time they interact with others they need detailed information. Thus, American business people (LC) often feel that French counterparts (HC) do not give them enough details, their messages are superfluous, they "talk in soufflés" and never get to the immediate point. French business people, on the other hand, report that the British and Americans are too pragmatic, fact obsessive, and abrupt. Their messages are so detailed that they are devoid of any "real" meaning.

These differences in message expectations and behavior are quite apparent during a "business lunch." In high-context cultures, the business lunch provides an essential context to develop and maintain appropriate relationships with people previously not part of one's network. The business lunch is a context that helps each person gain enough information about the other to be able to predict how they will behave and communicate in the future. It develops informal channels that will be used at a later date. Thus, appropriate topics may include politics, novels, latest movies, and fine foods, but not the direct business at hand. That will come later, after a relationship has been developed. Low-context cultures, on the other hand, tend to view lunch as a time to continue with the cold details of work and conduct "real business over lunch." Messages are directed at business and lots of facts and details are exchanged. No wonder American executives return from France filled with horror stories of all the time wasted (the average time spent at a French business lunch is 124 minutes) and the French return secure in their belief that Americans are brusque, uninteresting, and obsessed with work (the average business lunch in the United States is 67 minutes) (Adler, 1991).

create, desire, and understand. For example, Edward T. Hall (1980) distinguishes among cultures by the development, extensiveness, and interconnectedness of communication networks. According to Hall, context is the information that surrounds a message. Cultures with highly interconnected networks operate as high-context message producers; cultures with segmented and compartmentalized networks operate as low-context message producers. A *high-context* communication or message is one in which *most* of the information is already in the person and the relationship while very little is in the coded, explicit part of the message. A *low-context* communication is just the opposite; that is, the mass of the information is vested in the explicit code.

Hall's work, and that of many sociolinguists, suggests that message qualities are highly contingent upon network qualities. Consider the conversation between two second-year employees who have grown up in the same neighborhood, gone to the same high school, were in the same sorority in college, and now live two blocks apart. Often, their conversation will make little sense to those who are not part of their closely connected network. Their referents may not be clearly explicated, many details are explicitly left out, common terms have idiosyncratic meanings, and even the pace and rhythm of the conversation may seem strange. In contrast, the messages exchanged by people who have simple relations and communicate only about task-related concerns will be far more structured and explicit; background information will be provided and referents will be more clearly delineated. When attention is paid to the embeddedness of individuals, messages may be formulated and modified in ways that will increase the likelihood of the message being interpreted in the way the sender hopes it to be.

## MESSAGES HAVE MULTIPLE LEVELS

According to Stohl and Redding (1987), each message has four levels. Levels 1 and 2 deal with the *intentions of senders*, what is desired and intended; level 3 represents the *ostensive message*, what is actually verbalized; and level 4 delineates the *receivers' interpretations*. There are often important differences between levels. For example, level 1 represents what communicators would really like to say, in the absence of all constraints (e.g., "Boss, you really don't know what you're talking about"); level 2 captures what they decide they should say ("There may be some other opinions about that issue"); level 3 depicts what they do say ("Sir, that certainly seems to be an interesting possibility"); and level 4 indicates what the message means to the receiver ("That worker always is trying to show she knows more than me").

It is important to remember that not all messages are intentional. There are many times when we are perceived to have meant something by our actions that we do not intend. An employee who wears "inappropriate" dress to the Christmas party may not be making a protest statement even though others suggest he is; a pregnant employee may take her career very seriously, despite what meanings others put to her pregnancy; and the choice to sit alone in the cafeteria may not mean a person is unsociable, rather he may just be extremely busy.

---

## MAKING CONNECTIONS

During Ronald Reagan's two presidential terms, the media described him as "The Great Communicator." But, as this 1987 *Newsweek* story demonstrates, the lack of coordination among his network of advisers resulted in several unintentionally ambiguous messages that had serious ramifications for the nation. William Casey, who became CIA director under Reagan, was reported by *Newsweek* to be quite dismayed as the Reagan cabinet selection went forward after the election in 1984.

"Three names went forward for each cabinet post, and he [Casey] was on for [Secretary of] State and Defense. But there was no overall coordinator for top appointments, only pockets of authority. Things got screwed up terribly and quickly. Reagan had decided finally that George P. Schultz, the former Nixon and Ford cabinet member, was his first choice for State. Apparently thinking the groundwork had been laid, Reagan called Schultz. The trouble was that Schultz had been told he was on the Treasury list.

" 'I'm interested in having you join my cabinet,' Reagan said with unintentional ambiguity.

"Schultz, assuming it was Treasury, turned it down.

"Mike Dever, who was in the room when Reagan made the call, didn't learn until months later what had happened. Schultz would have accepted State. Reagan's second choice, Alexander Haig, emerged as the front runner" ("The Secret Wars of the CIA," 1987, p. 48. From *Newsweek*, Oct. 5, 1987, Newsweek, Inc. All rights reserved. Reprinted by permission).

In addition to the fallacy of believing all messages are intentional, many of us also assume that senders intend their messages to be clear and relevant. We presuppose people intend to say something sensible and understandable. However, people are sometimes strategically ambiguous. They intentionally produce messages that do not have one clear and definite meaning but are purposefully open to several interpretations. For example, telling a worker, in public, that her suggestion will be considered with "all the seriousness it deserves" can placate the worker who is anxious for her voice to be heard while reassure supervisors who may be threatened by participation. Being aware of the potential meanings embedded in messages helps individuals be more astute participants and effective communicators.

## MESSAGES HAVE MULTIPLE MEANINGS

In the previous section, we discussed how networks account for people's meanings and their ideas and conceptions about messages in general. Indeed, a major misconception about messages, *there is only one correct interpretation,* is often rooted in the homogeneity of a person's network. That is, when people frequently communicate and are enmeshed in a highly interconnected network, they tend to receive the same information and reading of a social situation over and over again.

*Weak ties often produce a more complex and complete view of information.*

This redundancy reinforces the view that there is only one correct way to interpret messages and events. In contrast, when a person has a number of weak ties (i.e., people whom they may not often communicate with and who are not linked to many others in their own network), they often receive new and unique information. The diverse set of opinions, rationales, and positions suggests there is more than one view of the situation. Weak ties often produce a more complex and complete view of information and messages.

Researchers in organizational communication have long been aware of the "gap" in understanding and/or information among

*need access
wide
to different
meanings*

specified homogeneous groups in organizations such as between management and labor, supervisory and hourly workers, rank and file union members and union headquarters staff. Tompkins (1962) termed this disparity of interpretation *semantic information distance*. Typically we assume that people in organizations have similar attitudes because they are enmeshed in *cohesive* groups, talking directly to and influencing one another. However, some network analysts have shown that *structurally equivalent* individuals (i.e., people who have no direct links with one another but who tend to have similar patterns of relations within systems) are more likely to hold similar attitudes.

Although seemingly contradictory, these network explanations of structural cohesion and structural equivalence are not mutually exclusive. Both help clarify how our networks influence frames of reference, message creation, and message interpretation. The first explanation is rooted in the power of direct communication between people. The second explanation is based upon the power of indirect yet similar communication experiences. Both can help us understand why union members may fear a "sellout" when their officials go meet with the management in fancy hotels; home office managers are often afraid their multinational manager will go "native" and no longer do what is best for the company; and spouses become fearful that they will be unable to communicate with their partners once they receive that big promotion.

In general, the more experiences a person has both inside and outside the organizations, the more likely he or she will be aware of the possibility of multiple interpretations of messages. Someone who has traveled extensively may not be immediately insulted when an English colleague asks to borrow "a rubber" at work. She is aware that such a request may refer to an eraser rather than a sexual act. On the other hand, her awareness of the potential for multiple meanings may make her sensitive to the possibility that the other person may be punning intentionally, and thereby make her even more suspicious of the ambiguity of the message. Stohl and Redding (1987) identify two different types of message ambiguity experienced by a receiver.

*Blatant ambiguity* occurs when a receiver is confused or uncertain about the meaning of a message. This may occur because the receiver cannot construct any plausible interpretation of the message (i.e., the message seems meaningless) or the receiver recognizes there are multiple possible meanings and cannot select or determine the intended meaning. When we have doubt as to what a message "means," we often seek out others in our network to help us interpret the message.

*Subtle ambiguity* occurs when there are two or more potential meanings to a message but the receiver is unaware of this possibility. For example, you go home and show your spouse the "wonderful" memo informing you of your new position. You interpret this message as an omen that bodes well for your future promotion. Your spouse, however, sees a different meaning in the message. If this was good news, why didn't the boss tell you herself, why was it put in impersonal memo form? Second, she or he points out that in this new assignment you are being isolated, taken away from the main flow, out of the centralized network. Rather than interpreting this message to mean that a new promotion is on the way, a counter-explanation is given. Who is right? Clearly, as an organizational insider you may have greater knowledge as to whether the "memo" form is standard operating procedure for this type of announcement, whether the others you will work with are on the inside track, and so on. What this example illustrates, however, is that even when a message may seem clear cut to one person, it may not be to another. In other words, ambiguity does not necessarily reside in the ostensive message itself but may be located in the source's intentions, the receiver's interpretations, the relationship, and/or the situation itself.

> *Ambiguity does not necessarily reside in the message but may be located in the source's intentions, the receiver's interpretations, the relationship, and/or the situation.*

From the sender's point of view, message ambiguity may be either negative or positive. Traditionally, the ideal message was assumed to be one that was absolutely clear, faithfully transmitted with complete fidelity and accuracy. From this standpoint, all messages are ostensive, they are assumed to have physical and spatial properties, that is, "real" things that can be used to transfer identically feelings and thoughts of one person to another. In an interesting study of managerial and organizational assumptions about messages, Axley (1984) points out that this *"conduit metaphor"* has embedded within it several assumptions about communication that are extremely problematic. For example, if a manager believes that successful communication "simply" entails the transmission of thoughts and feelings into words, there will be little focus or expenditure of time and resources upon

---

### MAKING CONNECTIONS

In 1989 an Avianca jet crashed approaching John F. Kennedy airport killing 73 of the 158 people aboard. The jet, flying in stormy weather, had aborted a first landing approach and was preparing for another attempt when it crashed into a New York suburb northeast of the airport. The United Press International (UPI) report at the time of the crash highlights the serious dangers of message ambiguity and points to the importance of communication training.

"The investigation hinged on exactly what words the crew used to describe the low fuel situation to controllers," Lee Dickson, a member of the National Transportation Safety Board said. Dickson said recorded tapes of cockpit conversations revealed that crew members never used the word *emergency* but did say they needed *priority* when making their second landing attempt after aborting the first.

UPI reported that when pilots declare a fuel emergency the situation is considered very serious and the plane is given priority to land over all other waiting planes. The air traffic control manual has no listing under terminology for a "fuel priority."

Tony Dresden, a spokesman for the National Air Traffic Controllers Association, the controller's union, was reported to have read transcripts of cockpit conversations and stressed that the Avianca pilot never declared an emergency.

"This guy never said he was in trouble. He didn't declare a fuel emergency. He didn't even say he had minimum fuel. Those are two keys. If he had said either one of those two, it would have been a whole different ball game." Asked what might have happened if the Terminal Radar Approach Control (TRACON), the system that handles approaches to land in Kennedy airport, had been aware of the Avianca emergency, Dickinson told UPI reporters TRACON may have taken different steps (United Press International, 1990, p. 9. Reprinted by permission of United Press International, Inc.).

actual communication processes within the organization. Such a view promulgates the idea that all a manager has to do is carefully tell a worker precisely what she means and it will get done. A more effective conceptualization of messages recognizes that communication does not involve the direct transfer of meaning, rather it is a process of interpretation and inevitable transformation. Message change, therefore, is not necessarily negative or the result of intentional wanton acts of distortion but an inherent part of the interpretive process.

Message ambiguity, and the resultant plethora of meanings attached to a specific message, may also be intentional and not the result of some inadvertent serial transmission effect. People often use ambiguity in a calculated manner. Communicative competence entails the strategic and oftentimes ambiguous use of symbols to accomplish specific goals. Effective bureaucrats can say absolutely nothing in so many words. Sensitive yet truthful friends can save your face by indirection. Brand-new, yet savvy employees will equivocally set up their position on a controversial issue until they understand the political nature of their response. Newly installed political appointees often have to learn to "mumble with great coherence" after being chided by other government officials for being too candid. Washington insiders often respond to questions with the well-known quip, "If I seem unduly clear to you, you must have misunderstood what I said" (*Newsweek*, Nov. 14, 1991).

The acknowledgment that once officials are appointed they can no longer speak for themselves, but instead represented the interests of the government through their own words, highlights an important but often unacknowledged characteristic of messages. That is, many organizational messages, although vocalized by an individual, do not represent an individual voice. Organizational messages often involve the management of multiple identities and multiple interests. They are not created nor can they be interpreted in isolation from the interlocking networks that join organizations and their publics (Cheney, 1991).

Eisenberg (1984) explicated several conditions under which organizational actors are likely to use *strategic ambiguity*. These include situations in which (a) people are faced with multiple and sometimes conflicting goals, (b) conditions are volatile and likely to change, (c) relations are tenuous, and (d) elite positions are somewhat threatened. Strategically ambiguous messages, Eisenberg illustrates, may promote unified diversity, allowing different interest groups to interpret symbols in ways that are consistent with their own values and beliefs without ever having to recognize the incompatibility or conflict of the multiple positions.

Further, strategically ambiguous messages facilitate change and creativity insofar as the messages provide flexibility for response. For example, in the chapter on participation, we discuss how in the 1980s organizations across the globe pledged themselves to increasing worker participation. Mission statements were crafted to commit all levels of the organization to work toward increased participation. What this commitment meant, however, was interpreted differently by people across the

---

### MAKING CONNECTIONS

A ubiquitous type of message that has not been closely examined in the organizational context is joking. Yet joking is a common form of message behavior that allows the speaker to disassociate him- or herself from the overt message by masking intention. For example, employees often joke with their bosses rather than openly challenge a manager's decision—if they are called on the challenge, they can say "only joking." Supervisors often use a joking message style to soften the tone of the command. Teasing, sarcasm, and joke telling are all ways of getting a point made, without being responsible for the message.

The ambiguity of humorous messages may deteriorate into a form of harassment, however. In a survey of 13,000 federal employees, the most prevalent form of sexual harassment was "unwanted sexual teasing" (Bureau of National Affairs, Inc., 1988). *Cockburn* (1991) highlights the problem in the following true story, which begins with the opening remarks of a senior manager to his staff at a weekend conference.

" 'We are lucky to have [the director] with us this morning. He's just risen from a sick bed. [Pause] His secretary has the flu.' This drew a laugh not only from the audience but from the director—and from his secretary who was present as well. Subsequent speakers followed with other sexual allusions and jokes. Many of the women and some men who were present at the meeting, and a number of employees who heard of it afterward were deeply offended and wrote a letter of complaint to the director, indicating that the jokes constituted a form of sexual harassment" (p. 146).

*(continued)*

workplace. For some, it meant limited activities designed to improve quality, health, and safety conditions by using employee suggestions; for others, it meant intensive involvement in strategic decision making.

Message ambiguity also may contribute to the preservation of privileged positions. People in power want to be careful that they do not limit their immediate or future options or preclude the possibility of reinterpreting the meaning of past communication. Messages are often carefully constructed so that people can later deny culpability for actions. In the classic text on organizational communication *Is Anybody Listening?* by W. H. Whyte Jr, the following maxim is presented: "All you have to remember is . . . let the language be ambiguous enough that if the job is successfully carried out, all credit can be claimed, and if not, a technical alibi can be found" (Whyte, 1952, p. 52).

Further, ambiguous messages may not only protect our positions but they also insulate us from facing the implications of our

---

A central question for employers and employees alike is the extent to which messages such as jokes, rather than behavior, such as unwanted touching, may constitute harassment. In 1987 the Equal Employment Opportunity Commission (EEOC) issued a set of harassment guidelines suggesting that derogatory remarks and joking about a person's age might violate the Age Discrimination in Employment Act of 1967. Joking about a person's sex, race, or ethnic origin may also be considered illegal harassment.

But there are great difficulties in determining whether these messages indeed constitute harassment. The disclaimer, "No, that's not what I meant at all," addresses only one level of message analysis and hence provides a very limited understanding of the potential meanings of the message. The director who received the above complaint admitted that perhaps the joke was inappropriate but justified his colleague's actions by suggesting that the response was blown completely out of proportion; after all, the comment was merely an attempt at humor.

In discussing these frictions, *Duncan, Smeltzer,* and *Leap* (1990) capture the essence of the problems and complexity of message analysis: "It is difficult to draw the line between joking behavior that is a natural part of workday life and behavior that constitutes sex, race, or age discrimination. To what extent are racist, sexist, and age related jokes likely to create a hostile work environment? When does humor become vicious and insulting? What types of conduct between the initiators, targets, focus, and public(s) are apt to create liabilities for an employer?" (p. 269).

own actions. Euphemisms, for example, are a special type of message that substitutes more pleasant expressions for ones that are offensive or unpleasant. Companies don't fire 200 people, they merely downsize. Offensive products are relabeled to mitigate their use. Armaments manufacturers don't talk about how many people their products can kill but highlight their ability to defeat "soft targets," and killing becomes the "arbitrary deprivation of life." Many onerous jobs are given more pleasant-sounding titles, for example, garbage persons become sanitary engineers, janitors are maintenance supervisors.

Not all organizational doublespeak is done to exert power and hurt. At times ambiguity may be well intentioned. Subtle and indirect messages may be designed to soften the blow of bad news, make you less uncomfortable hearing unpleasant news, or allow the person to say something without direct confrontation. Indeed, across situations and relationships, there is a pervasive systematic bias on the part of people to transmit messages that are pleasant rather than unpleasant (what Tesser & Rosen, 1975, call the MUM effect—keeping *Mum* about *Unpleasant Mes-*

---

### MAKING CONNECTIONS

One of the most famous cases of *plausible deniability*, a specific type of strategic ambiguity, has been attributed to President John Kennedy. Since 1962 there has been much speculation as to whether or not John Kennedy knew that the CIA plan he approved to invade Cuba included the plan to assassinate Fidel Castro, the Communist leader of that small Caribbean nation. In the book *Can Governments Learn? American Foreign Policy and Central American Revolutions* (1985), Lloyd S. Etheridge presents the reader with several arguments for each side of the issue. Of most concern here are the communication accounts that suggest that President Kennedy may not have "really" known, an argument that is based on the ambiguity of messages and the intentional creation of plausible deniability.

"Arthur Schlesinger Jr. presents the best brief for Jack Kennedy and his brother Robert, arguing that the assassination approval was a misunderstanding, one of those odd mix-ups. Everyone would know, Schlesinger says, that a "king can do no wrong" code (plausible deniability) should govern any discussions. The president always needed deniability and so he could not utter the exact words of approval himself: magically, by this

*(continued)*

sages). When people are asked to relay "news" to a stranger, an acquaintance, good friend, or co-worker via any media (e.g., phone, form letter, postcard, face-to-face), good news tends to be communicated more frequently, more quickly, more fully, and more spontaneously than bad news. The lack of transmission of bad news messages is found to be associated with the sender's own position, guilt, and mobility aspirations, the concern with the recipient, and normative proscriptions.

## MESSAGES ASSUME MULTIPLE FORMS

As the above discussion indicates, to understand organizational messages is a very complicated affair. It is even more complex when we consider the variety of forms that messages take, written or oral, mediated (e.g., via computer) or direct (e.g., face-to-face), verbal or non-verbal, formal or informal.

Let's imagine for a moment that you receive the following written message: *There will be an informal meeting on Tuesday to discuss options for a new health care facility on the work premises.* This

---

theory, he was not exactly 'tied' to what would follow if he communicated what he wanted without saying it in so many words. Knowing the code, no one would 'embarrass' a president by asking him directly, thereby compromising him if he said yes. A president and his CIA chief (who, it was understood, would take the rap) could also then testify, under oath if necessary, there has been no formal approval for such an operation

"By Schlesinger's theory, Allen Dulles [then CIA director] played a too subtle game with the president when they met in private and misunderstood his response. There is no manual for new presidents indicating that when a CIA director says, for example, that he is also discussing alternative ways to 'eliminate' Castro by providing financial support to private groups who have similar purpose (or whatever euphemism might be used), alarm bells should ring in the president's head and he should anticipate that assassination plans will shift into high gear unless he, at that moment, is alert enough to grasp what has just gone past him."

It is interesting to note that in these discussions of plausible deniability a distinction is made between insiders (those who know the code) and outsiders (those who don't). For plausible deniability to work, each member of the conversation must be aware of the unwritten rules and implicit codes of message production.

message seems very straightforward. You are a very strong supporter of the facility and have put in hundreds of hours researching the issue, coming up with several alternative models, and so on. You also know that this is a very controversial subject and are very pleased to discuss this in an informal setting, rather than in what you had feared, a big meeting in the lecture hall with 400 people, many of them hostile. So you prepare your remarks, but knowing this is just an informal meeting you don't have any strategy sessions with other supporters, you save the graphics for when it really counts, you have the information in your head. You have interpreted this "informal" meeting as a beginning, a context designed to get people to begin talking about the issue and you don't want to overwhelm anyone or appear too strident. You change into comfortable clothes, have a snack, and go to the meeting hall. You get there and are (a) surprised that everyone is wearing business suits, (b) a bit flustered to see the slide projector, and (c) dismayed because there is a large group of people from both inside and outside the company whom you know are against the project sitting together at a conference table with prepared data sheets and so on. Have you been tricked? Were you intentionally set up for failure? What went wrong?

In addition to the fact that, by relying completely on the written message and thereby acting in isolation, you missed out on obtaining relevant information about the purpose of the meeting, possible hidden agendas, the format, and so on, you didn't recognize that the formal/informal dichotomy is one of the most overused and non-exclusive category schemes for messages. In the above context, for example, *informal* was interpreted in the sense of message channel, social setting, structure, and format. Yet, what the memo's *informal* referred to was simply the absence of public commitment. This meeting was a trial balloon, informal in the sense that no official commitment would be made, but very important in that this was setting the foundation for decisions that would be formalized later. If you had known what types of messages were expected in this "informal" setting, you might have been far more prepared.

One of the most common uses of the terms *formal* and *informal* in organizations refers to communication networks themselves.

The formal network, operationalized in the organizational chart, reflects prescribed patterns for officially sanctioned messages. The informal network comprises spontaneous, emergent patterns resulting from discretionary choices of the individual.

A special type of informal network, defined by the nature of the messages that take place *(rumors)* within the network, is the grapevine. Being part of the organizational grapevine often makes a person feel included and somewhat powerful. Within any grapevine there are several individuals who regularly function as liaisons and these people often have higher unofficial status. Informal associations allow a person to link several clusters of people across functional lines and are developed both inside the organization and with persons outside the company, from employees at other locations and individuals not associated in any way with the firm. The grapevine, like other organizational networks, can only be understood in a context larger than one constrained by organizational boundaries. The grapevine is often a community phenomenon; it crosses hierarchical levels, functional roles, and professional affiliations.

---

### MAKING CONNECTIONS

*Chester Barnard,* a successful executive with AT&T and in government service, is often credited with being the first organizational theorist to focus directly on the central role of communication. He believed that communication must occupy a central place in any exhaustive theory of organizations "because the structure, extensiveness, and scope of organizations are almost entirely determined by communication techniques" (Barnard, 1938/1960, p. 91) Barnard defined an *organization* as "a system of consciously coordinated activities or forces of two or more persons."

Barnard's classic text, *The Functions of the Executive* (1938/1968), was written in response to his failure to find adequate explanation of his own executive experience in classical organization theory. Barnard acknowledged that alongside the formal structure of organizations existed a shadow world, an informal organization. "When formal organizations come into operation they create and require informal organization." The "personal contacts and interactions" of the informal organization "are necessary to the operation of formal organizations as a means of communication, of cohesion, and of protecting the integrity of the individual" (p. 104). For an organization to exist, there must be people who (a) are able to communicate with one another, (b) are willing to contribute action, and (c) have a common purpose.

Rumors can be conceptualized as sets of messages in general circulation lacking certainty as to their truth. They arise in and explain confusing and anxiety-producing events, thereby flourishing in an atmosphere of secrecy and competition. Rumors travel the corridors of an office or the length of a production line as soon as some new, confusing event occurs and creates an atmosphere of uncertainty. Closed door meetings are almost certain to produce a flood of rumors in times of uncertainty; personnel changes provide grist for the rumor mill. Rumors, traditionally communicated orally, can now also be found on electronic mail systems, computerized bulletin boards, and even the FAX machine.

Although many see the grapevine as presenting the greatest communication challenge to managers, the messages that travel within this informal network often serve management's interests quite well. Rumors are not nearly as inaccurate as some might believe. Messages in the grapevine travel quickly so it is a swift, cheap way to disseminate information (Rosnow & Fine, 1976). In other words, rumors, like all messages, serve multiple functions for individuals and organizations.

---

### MAKING CONNECTIONS

Grapevine communication usually emerges out of the social and personal interests of employees rather than the formal requirements of the organization. Thus grapevine topics are more often people oriented than issue oriented. At times these rumors have to do with how someone was stabbed in the back.

In most accounts of back stabbing, there are only three people: the person who is stabbed (i.e., the person whom the message is about), the person who has done the stabbing (the sender of the message), and the person who receives the message. However, Jeffrey Harvey, a professor of management, in a 1989 article titled "Some Thoughts About Organizational Backstabbing: Or, How Come Every Time I Get Stabbed in the Back My Fingerprints Are on the Knife?" argues that back stabbing is not simply a linear process of message sending and receiving but can only occur with the collusion of several people in your network. In reviewing the pattern of back stabbing, Harvey writes: *"Backstabbing is not a solitary crime committed by a solitary individual acting in isolation. Rather, it is an intricate kaleidoscope of collusive deception that involves the complicity of a wide variety of Perpetrators, Messengers, Witnesses, and the Victims."*

*(continued)*

## MESSAGES SERVE MULTIPLE FUNCTIONS

As suggested above, rumors are not the only messages that serve multiple functions. Our examples have shown how messages establish functional relationships through which individuals manage and coordinate their activities as they strive to accomplish personal, group, and organizational goals. Jargon, for example, serves to identify specific groups; mastering the restricted message code is essential for understanding a task and being a recognized member of the group. Feedback not only provides direction and/or stimulates greater effort, the messages define relational types.

The interpretation of the function of any given message is directly tied to the relationship between individuals. A manager

Back stabbing is a process that does not begin with the actual stabbing but starts when the potential victim hears a rumor from a third party, generally a trusted friend or associate, about the planned assault: "The messengers [the person(s) who is warning you] generally preface it by avowing their support for the Potential Victim and indicating their disrespect for the Potential Perpetrator. . . . Messengers also tend to begin or conclude their missives with an admonition such as 'This information must be held in strictest confidence.' Sometimes they buttress their restrictive covenants with elaborate and sensible sounding explanations as to why confidentiality is necessary to protect both the potential victim and themselves. Such demands for confidentiality frequently are supported by some version of the threat, 'If you use my name or even indicate to anyone else you know about this, I'll deny I ever said it and furthermore, I won't try and protect you from the Potential Perpetrator in the future.' Often the messenger also implicates several witnesses who know what is going on, but of course, this too is sworn to secrecy" (p. 273).

Harvey demonstrates how the potential victim, concerned about losing the support of his network (after all, these are his only friends who are telling him), does not do anything with the information. He can't confront the messenger and demand he stop it (that would make the messenger angry as well, and he is still an ally) nor can he act upon the knowledge in public. Ironically, once the potential victim agrees to the messenger's conditions (and how can he do otherwise?), the messengers and the victim become accomplices in the crime. The messengers (the friends in the network, by their silence and handcuffing the potential victim's options, become "side stabbers") and the victim, by failing to confront the potential perpetrator, helps to stab his own back. Back stabbing, then, like the rumors that precede and follow it, is enacted through the informal organizational network.

may say, "Please give me a report as soon as you can get to it" and mean, "I need that information in about a week" (a request for information), whereas the subordinate might interpret the message as, "Drop everything else and finish that report today" (a demand for action). Messages that are meant as simple declarations of fact by a person higher in the hierarchy ("I'll look into hiring another person for your group when things settle down with this account") are often interpreted by those lower in the hierarchy in a more evaluative manner ("I'm tied up with more important things, we'll forget about hiring indefinitely").

Understanding that messages can serve several of these functions simultaneously helps us make sense of what may seem like bizarre message behavior. For example, consider some of the more extreme cases of bureaucratic prose. Mitchell (1979) presents the very complicated official definition of an exit that goes on for pages in a government document. If we consider the definitional function is simply that of informing, the clumsily detailed and seemingly redundant message would be ridiculous. But if we consider the most important purpose of the message to be control (i.e., the stipulation of legal parameters for what constitutes an exit in a construction project), the message is no longer ridiculous and in fact meets the needs of the organization perfectly.

The *instrumental* use of messages to control another's actions is a fundamental aspect of organizational communication. Whether we are talking in a small group, giving a public lecture, having a brief conversation with co-workers in the hall, or conversing with our bosses, many of our efforts are devoted to regulating another person's behavior (influencing someone's ideas, actions, and behaviors) or persuading them (affecting their opinions, attitudes, or beliefs) and simultaneously maintaining good relations with the person. Power is traditionally defined as A getting B to do something he or she would not otherwise do (Dahl, 1961). Books like Dale Carnegie's classic *How to Win Friends and Influence People* (1981) and *Fighting It Out With Difficult—If Not Impossible—People* (Tucker, 1987) are best-sellers precisely because they appeal to a variety of audiences with the same need to learn how to control others.

Within the traditional exploration of power in organizations, several typologies of influence messages have been developed. Messages have been categorized based upon the type of strategy a person intentionally uses to get the other to do what he or she wants. Individuals may use hard tactics, which include demanding, shouting, and making assertive and threatening statements. Soft tactics are quieter and include flattering, ingratiation, and being nice. Rational tactics use logic and bargaining to demonstrate why compliance or compromise are the appropriate solutions (Kipnis & Schmidt, 1982).

The choice of message strategy has been shown to be based upon several factors that are consistent with the factors associated with most message behavior. The national culture of the participants influences their choice of strategies. Japanese tend

---

### MAKING CONNECTIONS

*Mary Parker Follett* (1868-1933) has been credited with being the first management consultant in the United States. Follett recognized that organizations are interdependent wholes. Her theory attempted to account for structural preservation as well as processes that cause organizations to change. She recognized that communication was not a linear process and that there are multiple causal loops that act simultaneously either to amplify or to counteract change. Her concern, like classical theorists, was with organizational control but her approach was quite different insofar as she emphasized the dynamic nature of interaction and message complexity. For example, in one paper, Follett concerned herself with *how* orders are given in the organization.

Follett (1941) argued that orders should arise from the situation so that both the "superior" and the "subordinate" are responding to the *"law of the situation,"* thus increasing the likelihood of compliance. She maintained that the organizational distance an order had to travel was inversely related to its effectiveness. In other words, an "order" delivered face-to-face was not only more efficient but also more effective than one issued in the upper echelons and left to work its way down the hierarchy. Face-to-face communication, Follett explained, created "circular" behavior, which served an integrating function within the system and allowed individuals to adapt mutually not only to each other but also to the constantly evolving organizational situation. Follett believed in the principle of *reciprocal response,* which suggests that communications between organizational members mutually and simultaneously influence one another. Her work is among the first to highlight the important role of worker participation, not only as a means to go along with management's wishes but as an actual process of mutual exchange and responsibility.

to use more indirect messages to influence; Indians rely more heavily on messages that emphasize one's dependency on the other (Pandey, 1986); and the Chinese are more likely to rely upon "obligation networks" and relationships with third parties to influence one another (Bond & Hwang, 1986).

The hierarchical positions of the message senders and targets affect the types of directives produced. People with less power tend to have fewer options, communicate in less diverse, more structured ways, and produce messages based primarily on appeals to rationality and expertise. People who are higher in the organizational hierarchy are able to enact more options although American managers typically use assertive, sanction-oriented, coercive messages (Fairhurst, Green, & Snavely, 1984). The psychological attributes of senders and receivers also influence message choice. People low in self-esteem and self-confidence have difficulty believing others will comply and so tend to use hard tactics. Overall, context is critical; if a person is "well connected," the sender is more likely to use "soft" tactics.

Although the above discussion may make it seem that compliance-gaining messages are unifunctional, they are not. What is perceived and designed as a demand for action may be interpreted by the target person as a request for information. Think

---

**MAKING CONNECTIONS**

*David Kipnis* and *Stuart Schmidt* are two researchers who have studied influence tactics in a variety of contexts. In an interesting study, Kipnis and Schmidt (1985) explore the influence tactics used by two of William Shakespeare's most famous characters, King Lear and Macbeth. They found systematic changes in the types of persuasive message strategies used by Lear and Macbeth during the five acts. As in their research with managers, workers, couples, and families, they found that in each play the choice of influence message strategies was related to the power base of the king. That is, when King Lear's power was at its peak (the beginning of the play), he uses hard influence tactics (coercive ones such as threats), but as his power decreases and he eventually loses his kingdom and his personal stature, his tactics become soft (including flattery). Macbeth, on the other hand, gains powers and a kingdom toward the end of the play. His tactics were equally distributed among the three types on the first two acts, but by the end of the play when Macbeth has consolidated his power and gained a kingdom, his tactics become increasingly hard.

back to a time when your mother or father told you were free to choose an option (perhaps if you would/would not join the family for a Sunday outing, or what you should/should not wear to the holiday dinner). When you did choose and told/showed him or her the results of your decision, you discovered (perhaps through non-verbal cues, coldness in tone or look, but rarely by a direct statement) that you had chosen the wrong alternative. What seemed to you to be a genuine request for information was actually a veiled directive for behavior. At that moment of realization, chances are you got very upset. By misunderstanding the function of the message, you obeyed and disobeyed the directive simultaneously—you couldn't win.

Indeed, people usually respond to contradictory messages with displeasure, frustration, confusion, and anxiety. In virtually all organized social systems, people receive mixed messages. Typical examples include the following: "Be independent and do what I say," "I order you to do what you want," "Give immediate notice when mistakes occur/You will be punished if you make a mistake," "Take the initiative/Don't break the rules," and "Think long term/Your present behavior will be punished/rewarded." Imagine you received a memo from

> *People usually respond to contradictory messages with displeasure, frustration, confusion, and anxiety.*

your boss, as one secretary did, that said, "There will be no overtime whatsoever," and then your boss comes to you and asks you to stay late to finish the report on his attempts to avoid overtime for all employees. Clearly, you have a problem. It is impossible for you to carry out his orders without violating his formal messages. To indicate the inconsistency will put your job at peril, as he can use it as evidence of insubordination.

Paradoxical messages, more than contradictions, embody an interactive struggle with opposites, an attempt to create meaning and coherence out of a set of messages that seem to defy such categorization. They are self-referential contradictory statements that create a vicious cycle with an emotional component (Putnam, 1985).

Messages such as "this is written in Japanese" are not paradoxical; they are contradictions and self-referential but do not
have the other two message qualities. The message from a department head, "I will not be taking attendance but I will be
taking down your name as you come in so I will know who to
introduce," will be more serious than funny for an untenured
faculty member with a time conflict, but it is not a paradox; it is

---

## MAKING CONNECTIONS

The double bind theory, proposed by *Gregory Bateson* and originally
developed to understand the etiology of schizophrenic behavior, makes no
distinction among types of social systems. Organizations as well as families
can meet the three criteria Bateson (1972) describes as essential for the
double bind: (a) The interactants are involved in an intense relationship in
which a person feels it is necessary to know what is being communicated
so that he or she can respond appropriately; (b) a person issues two orders
of message and one of these denies the other; (c) the individual is unable
to comment on the message being expressed, that is, she or he cannot
metacommunicate. In other words, a mixed message becomes a double
bind when the perceived inconsistency reveals a pattern of contradictions
that cannot be talked about. *R. D. Laing* (1970), a psychotherapist, has
written several poems that epitomize how the bonds of love, jealously, and
uncertainty are present in our messages. The patterns delineated illustrate
why we cannot comment upon the messages and so become prisoners of
these cycles. In his book *Knots*, Laing's poems represent several types of
relationships—lovers, parents and children, analyst and patient, boss and
workers. In each poem, once the message is verbalized, it is impossible to
get out of the cycle without completely changing the relationship.

1
They are playing a game. They are playing at not
playing a game. If I show them I see they are, I
shall break the rules and they will punish me.
I must play their game, of not seeing the game.

2
Jill:  You think I'm stupid.
Jack:  I don't think you're stupid.
Jill:  I must be stupid to think you think I'm stupid if you don't;
or you must be lying.
I am stupid every way:
to think I'm stupid, if I am stupid
to think I'm stupid, if I'm not stupid
to think you think I'm stupid, if you don't.

*Through comm. we try to make some kind of order out of all that ambiguity*

self-referential and contradictory and has an emotional component but does not create a vicious cycle. But imagine that you go to one manager complaining that you believe another manager has lied to you about a very important issue and you ask if what he said was true. The second manager replies, "Don't worry, it's not true, but you shouldn't be angry, all managers must lie to do their job." You go away thinking the problem is solved, but upon reflection, you begin to wonder, did manager 2 lie to you just to calm you down and keep you working or did she tell you the truth? This interaction is paradoxical: How can you work this out? Going to ask another manger doesn't help; if all managers lie, then you won't get the truth. Did the manager lie about all managers' lying? Almost any action you do within the system will simply continue the cycle. Putnam (1985) describes these paradoxical cycles as "perpetual oscillation between existent alternatives." To solve the paradox, one must transcend the system.

The explication of paradoxical messages leads to consideration of the *discursive power* of messages in organizations. Critical theorists persuasively argue that communication is never neutral. At the most fundamental level, messages are about power; they constitute networks of meaning and identity. Communication creates a context of rationality; the rules structure not only what is said but what cannot be said. Organizational messages thereby create and provide a context in which people learn to interpret what is possible, what is not possible, what is good and bad, what is valued and what is not valued (Mumby, 1988).

> *Communication is never neutral, it creates a context of rationality.*

## ❑ Final Connections

Messages are the complex matrix of symbols, interpretations, and responses that generate both formal and informal organizational networks. Messages are part of all organizational problems and solutions. This fundamental tension is easily seen in the various solutions to a common problem: information overload. *Overload* refers to the transmission of new information at a rate that far exceeds the input-processing and output-generating capabilities of individuals. Both maladaptive and adaptive responses are communicative in nature, which by their very nature transforms organizational networks.

For example, message overload may result in the intentional or unintentional modification of messages by omitting messages, modifying messages, and/or sampling messages. In each case the messages and patterns of message exchange are changed. A second type of response relates to network specialization. Relevant messages are redefined and delegated to others either in or outside the system, new priority systems are developed in which jobs are redefined so as to apply some selective criteria for message relevance or importance, and/or interpersonal networks are restructured so that there is decentralization and the creation of multiple channels. Each of these solutions makes it less likely that the individual will be saturated. In each of these solutions, the interpersonal bonds between persons may be loosened, dissolved, or redefined, and new attachments will develop. In other words, it is impossible to separate relationships from message phenomena; there is no sharp dividing line between sender and receiver. Thus we can see how to understand organizational messages we must understand the rich tapestry of relations that constitute our networks. Such an understanding evokes several paradoxes: *Message senders are simultaneously receivers, receivers are simultaneously senders; message redundancy is necessary, though overload must be controlled;* and *the messages sent are never the messages received.*

# Relationships

*The last chapter addressed the interdependence among mes-*
*sages, relationships, and meanings by focusing directly upon*
*message phenomena. This chapter highlights relationships,*
*the complex tapestry of associations, affiliations, and alle-*
*giances that weave together our personal networks.*

Relationships are an essential component of organizations. As
emphasized in the previous chapters, messages "make sense" in
terms of our relationships and identifications with others. Our
status, power, and even the trust people have in us is determined,
in part, by our personal connections. The three general characteristics of organizational conflict—interaction, interdependence,
and incompatible goals (Putnam & Poole, 1987)—are situated in
the relationships people develop with one another. Ethical
choices are strongly influenced by our association with others.

The term *looking-glass self* aptly reflects important features of
relationships (Cooley, 1902). Self-concept, self-respect, and a gen-

eral sense of well-being are rooted in our relationships. Informal
social support networks and increasingly popular self-help groups
provide relationships that help people buffer and share stress and
pain. If someone asks you to describe yourself, it would be impossible to do so without describing your personal relationships.

This chapter focuses directly upon relationships, a basic unit
in our view of organizations as "connectedness in action."

Even though most networks contain more than 2 people and more
than a single relationship, in actual functioning only *one dyad* and
*one relationship* are activated at any one moment in time. The basic
unit in the network remains a dyad, the members of which interlock

---

### MAKING CONNECTIONS

Personal relationships constitute important organizational resources.
The following account illustrates how an organization's ability to "scoop"
its competitors had little to do with its formal communication structure
and a great deal to do with the personal network of one of its lower level
employees.

On Thursday, June 12, 1986, the American Broadcasting Corporation
ran an interview with Barbara Walters and the Duvaliers (the exiled
Haitian dictators who had stolen or misappropriated millions of dollars).
News organizations throughout the world had tried to get interviews with
the Duvaliers in France and all had been unable to arrange it. According
to the *New York Times* (June 29, 1986), ABC was able to arrange an interview
partially because they had obtained several documents to which the
Duvaliers wanted to respond. These included copies of signed checks as
well as other papers "showing how the Duvaliers had money transferred
from the National Defense fund of Haiti to private accounts. There was
one document showing that a million dollars had been taken from the fund
and handed over to the Duvaliers' interior decorator."

How did ABC get these powerful documents and hence "scoop" their
competitors? *They used personal relationships that were outside the organizational context.* Specifically, through informal organizational channels, ABC
researchers "learned that the law firm representing the Government of
Haiti against the Duvaliers was Stroock, Stroock, and Lavan." A young
researcher, who worked for ABC, Jessica Stedman, "remembered that a
friend from Harvard was a nephew of the founder of the law firm. She got
in touch with him," and he made connections with one of the firm's
partners. Jessica and Joe Lovett, a producer at ABC, visited the firm. The
documents were obtained and the Duvaliers consented to the interview
(Walters, 1986, pp. 1, 15H. Copyright © 1986 by The New York Times Company. Reprinted by permission).

their behaviors relative to the particular components of the task. (Lipnack & Stamps, 1986, p. 98)

The increasing diversity of the American workplace has complicated organizational relationships in several ways. Specifically, the influx of women, racial and ethnic minorities, and people with non-traditional lifestyles has seriously called into question the conventional ways of communicating and doing business. Men and women who have not shared in the same types of experiences and/or have different cultural backgrounds "see" and experience the world differently. They have divergent expectations about how work should get done, what is appropriate behavior, and how problems should be solved. These differences can result in more creative, flexible, synergistic systems or they can be costly for individuals and organizations in terms of lost time, turnover, and unproductive conflict. People tend to be most comfortable communicating with others like themselves (Gudykunst, 1991). Individuals who resent and feel threatened by difference are often fearful of losing power. Under these circumstances, they can sabotage organizational relationships, assuring that the "outsiders" fail.

To answer the relational challenges inherent in a diverse workforce, many organizations have begun "Managing Cultural Diversity" programs. More than 50% of the *Fortune* 500 companies have diversity departments that are charged with facilitating relationships among the workforce by reducing stereotyping, increasing cultural sensitivity, improving employee communication skills, and providing mentors and access to informal networks (Jackson, 1992, p. 3).

An emphasis on relationships has permeated organizational thinking in other ways as well. The introduction of new communication technology is viewed by many in relational rather than technical terms. Multinational corporations have spent millions of dollars on computer technology intended to keep people in touch with one another. Electronic mail systems are designed to provide flexible, informal channels that facilitate relational development across great geographic distances (Guterl, 1989). According to a senior vice president at Texas Instruments:

You delude yourself if you think that the emphasis on technology transfer is on technology. It's a humanistic task, not a technical one. Stripped to its core, the task is to make sure that the right people are in contact with one another and supporting one another's efforts. (Bylinski, 1990, p. 73)

---

## MAKING CONNECTIONS

One of the most significant types of relational communication is "face-saving." *Face* refers to the "public self image that every member wants to claim for her/himself" (Brown & Levinson, 1978, p. 66). Face-saving is the act of preserving one's prestige and dignity. It is a means of protecting a credible image or avoiding a weak one (Goffman, 1967). The communication behaviors associated with losing or saving face vary across cultures as does the severity of negative consequences associated with losing face. Cultural diversity in the workplace has heightened the importance of sensitivity to "face" issues in organizational communication. When people lose face in a relationship, communication tends to become less productive.

Many managers from the United States (a low-context culture), for example, tend to be less concerned with face-saving than managers from high-context cultures. Communication and feedback are expected to be direct and specific. Although managers recognize the need to occasionally tell a "white lie" to allow both people in the relationship to save face, more likely the business person will favor direct confrontations, argumentation, and honesty with the other. Fairhurst et al. (1984) found that when confronted with poor performance many American supervisors initially attempted to use a problem solving, face-saving approach but would soon abandon it for a punitive approach, reverting to criticism, reprimands, threats, or orders.

In contrast, Mexican managers pay much closer attention to the relationship and avoid direct confrontation and negative interactions. A blunt no to a request, a direct countermand, or other blatant disagreements are seen as interpersonal rejections. According to Kras (1988), many Mexicans perceive their U.S. counterparts to lack "personal sensitivity." She suggests that managers from the United States "need to resist saying outright, 'You are wrong.' The Mexican knows perfectly well when he has made a mistake, but verbalizing it puts him to shame and is liable to make him withdraw" (p. 65).

In Japan, face-saving is so critical that managers and employees will use indirection and ambiguity so as to assure that a person does not unintentionally lose face. People who directly ask for a commitment or an opinion are considered rude because they force the other person to lie to save face. As a result, Japanese communicators use a "politeness strategy" in which the central issues of an argument are expressed implicitly rather than explicitly (Tirkkonen-Condit, 1988).

Clearly, our understanding of organizational communication must be based, in large part, upon our understanding of relationships. In this next section, we will closely examine the dynamics of these connections by focusing on five characteristics of relationships: (a) orientation, (b) multiplexity, (c) symmetry, (d) reciprocity, and (e) strength.

---

### MAKING CONNECTIONS

*Elton Mayo* was a central force among researchers at the Harvard Business School in the 1920s and 1930s. His work had a profound effect on what become the "Human Relations" school of management.

Mayo took issue with what he termed the "rabble hypothesis" infusing the classical management model—the notion that the worker is a rational, isolated individual acting only to maximize self-interest. Mayo countered this view with a more "humanistic" view of the worker as a social creature influenced by group norms and individual sentiments. Interpersonal relationships and communication as well as the attitudes and values of workers and management were strongly associated with organizational effectiveness.

Mayo (1933/1960) laid out his management model in his classic work, *The Human Problems of Industrial Civilization.* He makes the case that individuals are of indeterminate nature. That is, the worker is malleable and, given the correct rewards, can willingly adapt to almost any conditions. As a result, management can use education, alterations of the environment, and other inducements to shape and reshape the individual to fit the organization. Worker resistance was evidence of management's failure to identify and employ the proper inducements. Mayo assumed that enlightened managerial leadership would use inducements to shape workers in a benevolent fashion and provide an environment to take advantage of the workers' "eager human desire for cooperative activity." As a result, "new" organizations would arise wherein industrial workers could realize their human potential.

Mayo and the subsequent Human Relations Movement is widely criticized on several fronts: They tend to emphasize psychological explanations to the exclusion of objective conditions within the organization. The view that management is "enlightened and benevolent" seems somewhat naive and fails to consider both the relations of power in organizations and the potential for manipulation and exploitation. Somewhat averse to competition and conflict, this work tends to overlook the potential benefits of conflict as well as the downside of pervasive organizational harmony. Nonetheless, the Human Relations school continues to strongly influence contemporary models of "participative management."

## ❏ The Dynamics of Relationship

A relationship is a connection between two people. The relationship may be mediated or direct, intimate or distant, publicly acknowledged or private. We most often describe relationships in terms of kinship patterns (my brother-in-law, his cousin), degree of intimacy (acquaintance, friend, lover), role relations (boss, co-worker, fellow traveler), and organizational affiliations (classmate, ACLU member) (Knapp, 1984). A defining characteristic of many relationships is their position within a larger network. For example, a friend of a friend may feel comfortable asking us for a favor based solely upon our connection to our common friend. Someone we see and talk to every day at the office may remain nothing more than an acquaintance, despite an obvious attraction, because he or she is the supervisor's daughter or son.

*A defining characteristic of many relationships is their position within the larger network.*

RELATIONAL ORIENTATION

Historically, sociologists distinguished between two distinct relational orientations: *expressive* and *instrumental* (Parsons, 1951). These orientations mirror the traditional dichotomy between primary groups (e.g., family, clan) and secondary groups (e.g., the rational bureaucratic organization) and reinforce the "myth of separate worlds." Expressive ties were believed to be holistic, related to personal gratifications, and emotionally based, valued as ends in and of themselves. Instrumental ties, deliberate, limited in scope, and emotionally neutral, were indicative of those relationships arising in the course of performing appointed work roles.

These distinctions are helpful insofar as they highlight differences in relational expectations but, if taken literally, give us a false sense of organizational relationships. People do not shed their expressive selves when entering an organization. As the early Hawthorne experiments of the Human Relations Movement showed, expressive ties develop quite naturally in work groups, and these informal social relations strongly influence production standards, performance norms, and interpretations of managerial communication. The original analyses (Roethlisberger & Dickson, 1939) and subsequent reanalysis (Franke & Kaul, 1978) illustrate how the network of workers' social relations exerted strong pressure on members to limit their production in spite of a management incentive plan to produce more. The social networks helped to define workers' self-interest. These shared interpretations may have impeded the attainment of formal or-

---

### MAKING CONNECTIONS

Although the intentional development of relationships for instrumental purposes is a common occurrence in the United States, Americans tend to refrain from open discussion about these actions except in a disparaging manner. In other cultures, however, relationship development based upon specific instrumental goals is not only accepted but seen as a legitimate and appropriate way to do business and/or attain desirable resources.

In China, for example, the development of obligation networks called *Guanxi* or *kuan-hsi* is central to influence and compliance-gaining attempts. *Kuan-hsi* is used for getting more clients for one's business, solving conflicts, getting a job, and helping one's career (Hu & Grove, 1991).

The Chinese are said to pull *kuan-hsi* (*la kuan hsi*), manipulate *kuan-hsi* (*kao kuan-hsi*), or climb *kuan-hsi* (*p'an kuan-hsi*) to develop relations with others (Chang & Holt, 1991). Influence tactics include "using the back door," which refers to getting a person of higher status to intervene on your behalf, gift giving, doing favors, and providing social invitations to another to develop or climb *kuan-hsi*.

Chang and Holt discuss four ways of developing *kuan-hsi*:

(a) appealing to relatives, even quite distant ones;
(b) pointing out previous associations such as coming from the same geographic area or school;
(c) using intermediaries who already have *kuan-hsi* with the person one wishes to influence; and
(d) establishing social interactions by going to nightclubs and other social events.

*Guanxi* and *kuan-hsi* exchanges are not used in a cold or calculating manner but are seen as the "grease" that makes daily life run smoothly (Hu & Grove, 1991, p. 52). In fact, those who do not grant special treatment to those who attempt to establish *kuan-hsi* may be blamed for "lacking human feeling" (Chang & Holt, 1991, p. 260).

ganizational goals but clearly benefited workers in a time when an economic depression was in full force and workers across the country were losing their jobs.

Further, when people like their jobs, feel good about the place they work, and value their experiences at work, close expressive relationships are likely to arise. Rawlins (1992) states: "Indeed, if people are involved in, dedicated to, and derive personal esteem and/or social prestige from their occupation working with others and talking shop afterward are likely to combine self expression and emotional catharsis with instrumental accomplishment. Such relationships may become close friendships" (pp. 161, 162).

---

### MAKING CONNECTIONS

A significant change in today's workforce can be seen in what has been called the "new careerism." Graduates leaving college 30 years ago planned and expected to work in the same company, with the same people, for most of their careers (Whyte, 1956). Today's college graduates expect their "careers" to comprise a series of jobs that will likely involve several moves and engagement in and withdrawal from a multitude of networks. Employees realize that (a) organizations are volatile and it is unlikely employees will spend their whole lives in one organization, (b) organizations are not concerned with their employees' best interests, and (c) employees have to assume control of their own careers because no one will do it for them (Feldman, 1988).

An unintended consequence of this new careerism, according to Daniel Feldman (1988), is the development of *unauthentic interpersonal relationships* in the workplace, that is, *instrumental relationships devoid of all expressive content*. Feldman vividly explores the "pronounced me-first careerism in the managerial, academic, and professional community" and highlights what this has done to the social fabric of organizations.

"Concomitant with the lack of job involvement and organizational commitment is an increase in purely instrumental interpersonal relationships. Managers make little investment in getting to know their subordinates, subordinates make little effort to know their superiors and co-workers do not exert much energy getting to know each other. Independent of rank, everybody makes the same assumption; they will not be working with each other long enough to bother getting to know each other as people. In addition, purely instrumental relationships make it easier to be covert in one's career strategy. If we define our colleagues as people to whom we have commitments, then we will not constantly be job-searching or job-hunting—or at least we will not be doing so on the sly. If we define our relationships with colleagues as purely instrumental, we can give them no quarter and owe them no explanations" (pp. 207-208).

RELATIONAL MULTIPLEXITY

Links may vary in the degree to which they transcend any one orientation or network domain. *Uniplex* relationships remain within one domain. A business relationship in which the participants never talk about anything but work, and neighbors who only know the most banal and impersonal things about each other, are typical uniplex relationships. The term *multiplexity* refers to the overlap of contents, activities, and/or functions in the relationship. Specifically, a link is role multiplex if a person occupies more than one "designated" role for the other. A co-worker who is also your quality circle leader and a bridge partner represents a multiplex link. Content multiplexity captures the degree to which the content of the communication encompasses messages related to more than one domain; a link may represent communication about work, family, sports, and religion.

Multiplex relationships tend to be more enduring, intense, stable, influential, supportive, and intimate (Burt, 1983; Rogers & Kincaid, 1981). Albrecht and Hall (1991) suggest that people do not maintain highly multiplex relationships without high levels of certainty and trust. Multiplex links may also provide the individual with richer information than would otherwise be available. For example, friendships among group members outside a formal group context may affect internal deliberations in the organizational group. Members may be forewarned about the controversial positions of their friends or be able to sidestep potential crises because interpersonal histories help them know what the other will or will not tolerate.

Multiplex relationships constitute critical linkages in social support networks both within and outside the organization (Tolsdorf, 1976). Support networks "buffer" the individual from unwanted stress, provide material resources, furnish emotional outlets for venting frustrations and anger, give information and advice, provide linkages to others, and minimize burnout (Ray, 1987). Supportive relationships include an element of caring (Cobb, 1976) and/or the ability to help the person increase his or her sense of mastery and control over the environment (Albrecht & Adelman, 1984). Supportive networks create a safe place for people to share anxiety, concerns, interpretive ambiguities, and pleasures as well as provide individuals links to internal/external resources.

The most supportive relationships are often with those who can provide more than a sympathetic ear. The ability to provide opportunities to facilitate change is crucial. Workers with supportive supervisory relationships, for example, are less likely to experience stress than workers whose support networks comprise co-workers, friends, and relatives (House, 1981). Supportive co-workers may merely exacerbate feelings of helplessness, and reinforce negative feelings, if they do not have the knowledge, resources, or other power tools that would allow them to change the situation and provide instrumental support (Kanter, 1983).

> *Multiplex networks may cause as well as alleviate stress.*

Rich multiplex networks, however, may also cause as well as alleviate stress. For example, high levels of family and co-worker support are associated with higher levels of emotional exhaustion (Ray & Miller, 1991). The time it takes to develop and maintain highly multiplex networks can be overwhelming and add to the time pressures and burdens a person is already experiencing. Supportive relationships may become burdensome as the person is asked to reciprocate support and the "links become chains." Role conflict may be a direct result of multiplex relationships. Further, when someone becomes dependent upon another, the asymmetry of the relationship gives the other power, what may be called the "politics of supportive communication" (Ray, 1993).

Finally, a significant drawback of supportive multiplex relationships occurs when people become so closely identified with one another that they lose their individuality. Individual achievements may then be discounted, and a person's worth is devalued. The delicate balance between giving support and taking control and developing autonomy and creating dependence is perhaps nowhere more precarious than in what is the most formal and multiplex supportive relationship—mentor and protégé.

Multiplex relationships are also fraught with ethical dilemmas. The potential for role conflict is expanded when personal and work lives are enmeshed and decision making crosses domains.

---

### MAKING CONNECTIONS

Mentoring relationships are formally prescribed supportive multiplex relationships. Many organizations, such as Bell Laboratories, Federal Express, and the Internal Revenue Service, have started mentor programs (Fagenson, 1988) in the hopes that the special relationships will help socialize and assimilate the diverse set of employees now entering the workforce. The programs are designed to foster a sense of belonging and empower the mentoree.

Mentors are usually people of higher status who have been with the organization for a long period of time. The mentor relationship is specifically designed to help the new employee cope with four critical developmental issues: (a) learning the appropriate norms and "ways of doing" in the organization, (b) gaining knowledge and access to influential people, (c) understanding the composition of valued resources and attaining them, (d) being aware of important policy decisions and influencing them (Fagenson, 1988). Mentors look out for their mentoree, give advice on a regular basis, and bring the mentoree's accomplishments to the notice of others in the organization. Mentors may have several roles including (a) teacher, coach, or trainer; (b) role model; (c) developer of talent; (d) opener of doors; (e) protector; (f) sponsor; (g) promoter; and (h) supporter/counselor (Feldman, 1988).

Mentors help the new recruits secure opportunities by conferring approval, prestige, and backing as well as introducing them to people to whom they would not ordinarily have access. An important by-product of mentoring relationships is that personal networks are enriched. Employees who have mentors tend to perceive themselves as having more knowledge, influence over organizational policy, resource power, and access to important people than those without mentors (Daniels & Logan, 1983; Feldman, 1988)

But the mentor relationship, like other intense multiplex relationships, involves feelings of ambivalence and may set up several relational challenges. The mentoree is grateful for the opportunity to receive aid and advice but also wants to do it on his or her own. He or she is also aware that he or she needs to be perceived as an autonomous actor, not just "Danny's boy or girl." The time spent with the mentor is often very pleasant but he or she may want to make other friends and listen to and gain other perspectives. Mentors are also ambivalent. Being an effective mentor takes a great deal of time. Many mentors aren't sure the efforts provide significant rewards. Furthermore, too close an association with the new employee not only hinders the employee's ability to be his or her own person but may compromise the credibility of the mentor.

For example, the likelihood of blowing the whistle on corporate crime is decreased when the culprits are our friends or when we are involved with those who give silent sanction by looking away (Grabosky & Braithwaite, 1986). If someone is your friend and your boss, does she tell you about the likelihood of the plant closing when you are in the process of deciding whether to take a new job even when she is sworn to secrecy by the company's CEO? Which role takes priority when you are told something in strictest confidence as a friend that has significant implications in the workplace? Rawlins (1992) discusses the dialectical tensions inherent in relationships that transcend the private and public realms. "The ongoing rhetorical challenge to friends is to develop and share private definitions and practices while orchestrating desired social perceptions of the relationship" (p. 10). A network perspective makes us highly cognizant of the potential conflicts of interest situated in most multiplex relationships.

RELATIONAL SYMMETRY

Relationships may be *symmetrical* or *complementary* (Watzlawick, Beavin, & Jackson, 1967). That is, people may be joined together as equals or one may have greater power, prestige, prominence, and so on. Power is so embedded in organizational experience

---

**MAKING CONNECTIONS**

When *USA Today* reporter Doug Smith publicly confronted tennis star Arthur Ashe about the possibility that he had AIDS, the controversy between rights of privacy and the public's right to know was not the only issue that was raised. The ethical and emotional tensions embedded in multiplex relationships were brought to the forefront of the news. Journalists such as Bryant Gumbel of *The Today Show* and Frank DeFord of *Newsweek* magazine publicly admitted they had known for years that Ashe had AIDS (*Newsweek*, April 20, 1992, p. 63; *The Today Show*, April 11, 1992). Clearly, and understandably for most of us, their friendships with Arthur Ashe superseded their roles as news reporters. Each man chose not to go public with the information. Someone else, however, clearly did not hold such priorities. *USA Today*'s actions were a direct result of someone breaching a trust, a trust that, as public reaction to the disclosure indicated, should have been sacred. Although many did not blame *USA Today* (indeed, in some cases the editorial process was praised for its careful

*(continued)*

that the next chapter deals specifically with the structural mani-festation of complementary relationships—hierarchy. In this chapter, we will discuss more general concerns related to inter-personal dynamics.

Relational symmetry strongly affects message interpretations. For example, if your friend, also a team member, mentions how overworked she is on a given project, you may interpret that message as a call for help or sympathy or merely as tension relief. If the friend is also your boss, it is more likely you would interpret the message as a warning to reprioritize your own work and become more active in the project.

Symmetrical and complementary relationships embody differ-ent expectations regarding the types of message content that are appropriate as well as the degree and types of communicative control you can exert. If a colleague berates you in public, you may indicate your anger at him "being way out of line" while remaining somewhat bemused by his outrageous outburst. If your boss berates you publicly, you are more likely to feel angry *and* frustrated because you are unable to directly confront her inappropriate behavior for fear of later reprisals.

Recognition of the symmetrical or asymmetrical nature of a link is complicated by the fact that in American culture a pre-mium is put on warm, friendly relations. The egalitarian, coop-

confirmation of the information before going to press; see *Newsweek*, April 20, 1992), there was a great deal of outrage among the public that someone used personal information that may have "helped them do a job" but in a way that compromised Ashe.

On the other hand, there are many times when the decision to keep silent about information related to one's friends is considered outrageous and unethical. There is the infamous case of U.S. Representative Wilbur Mills, whose known alcoholism severely compromised his ability to do his job but didn't become public knowledge for years because his friends on Capitol Hill kept silent. The conspiracy of silence that surrounded several allegations in the savings and loan scandal and the Iran-Contra affair suggest that the dearth of whistle-blowers—that is, those who would call attention to organizational or individual malpractice—is not only the result of fear for one's job but the consequence of multiplex linkages. Friend-ship's code of silence does not necessarily lead to illegal activities or even unethical choices but the ethical dilemma is inherent in these multiplex relationships.

erative, cordial, and open style of communication practiced
across hierarchical levels belies the competitive, individualistic,
and bureaucratic approach to many professional affiliations. International colleagues, new employees, and minority workers
unfamiliar with the communicative norms of American organizations are often dismayed when they discover they have misin-
terpreted a co-worker's openness and familiarity; what they
perceived as actual friendship was merely the way Americans
deal with an acquaintance.

*Romantic relationships at work.* The complementary and symmetrical nature of relationships becomes especially salient, confused, and entangled when we consider sexual relations in the
workplace. Not only is romance in the workplace increasing as
more women enter the workforce, but as people delay marriage,
stay single longer, and divorce more often, there are more unmar-
ried people in the workforce. More than 25% of marriages result
from relationships begun at work (Hearn & Parkin, 1987).

Romantic involvement with co-workers has also become more
likely because increasing demands for teamwork and global
participation lead people to work closely together, spend long
and intense days and evenings finishing projects, and become
intimately involved with one another's work. Quinn (1980) reports that activities such as consulting, business trips, international conventions, and attendance at organizational social activities are a factor in 77% of all workplace romances. When
people become interdependent, need and rely on one another,
value each other's opinions, and share things they can't with
other people, romantic involvement becomes all the more possible (Neugarten & Shafritz, 1980). Further, as AIDS and other
security factors make the "singles" scene increasingly undesir-
able and dangerous, the workplace offers a safe, reliable meeting
place. Companies have typically handled sexual relationships
between employees in an unambiguous manner that reinforced
and even strengthened male dominance. That is, when a couple
became romantically linked, the woman was required to leave
the firm (Cockburn, 1991). Even today, when more women are in
higher level positions and there is a greater acceptance of work-

place romances, it is usually the woman who pays a greater price for the liaison. Ellen Rapp (1992) describes the outcome of an office affair between a female boss and her employee.

Last year, when a manager became involved with a subordinate in the public-affairs department of a small New England information-services company, it was the boss—a woman—who suffered more. The man's wife worked at the same firm in the benefits department. "She was very respected" says a source. In fact, all three of them were considered effective in their jobs. When news of the affair leaked out, "the boss ended up losing a lot of respect and credibility because support poured toward the wife," says the source. "Employees began snubbing the boss, placing nasty notes on her desk, even harassing her with phone calls. Her productivity was hurt." Eventually she grew so uncomfortable she left the company. . . . The unfaithful husband and the wife, however, are still in their same positions at the firm. (Rapp, 1992, p. 59; first appeared in *Working Woman*, February 1992. Reprinted with the permission of Working Woman magazine, copyright © 1992 by Working Woman, Inc.)

Romantic relationships have been defined as "intimate relationships characterized by some degree of mutual sexual attraction" (Dillard, 1987). In American culture, romantic relationships are assumed to be consensual and uncoerced. Romance assumes reciprocity and symmetry. In the workplace, however, such assumptions become problematic. When you have structurally nonequivalent relationships, how does one know if someone is feeling coerced? When one person has control over another, how can we know if the subordinate's actions are freely given? These relationships are so fraught with ambiguity, danger, and ethical problems that many organizations have rules explicitly discouraging the relationships.

The effect of workplace romances reverberates throughout networks. Communication within and across networks may change in several ways as co-workers become unofficial players in office romances. Romance can add excitement and interest to a dull office (Horn & Horn, 1982) and potentially increase coordination and improved work flow (Quinn, 1980). Romantic entanglements can also foster anxiety and suspicion. Members of the network may spend a great deal of time analyzing the couples' behavior. People may begin to withhold information as issues of territoriality, trust, and confidentiality become major concerns. Furthermore, people may begin to isolate the lovers to avoid having their own behaviors become suspect. For example, a manager in a large manufacturing plant stopped inviting co-workers to his house to avoid having his wife find out there was an affair going on at work. The manager felt that if his wife knew she would no longer trust him during his late nights at the office or on his business trips. His concern is reflected in the results of a large-scale study of romantic relationships at work which indicated that 22% of employees believe the establishment and visi-

---

### MAKING CONNECTIONS

As a result of several highly publicized sexual harassment cases and the subsequent increased public awareness, recent court decisions, and pressure from organized and ad hoc women's groups, organizations across the country are working on new sexual harassment guidelines. These guidelines must strictly adhere to and protect the rights of individuals while at the same time clearly define what is and is not acceptable behavior. In the case of consensual relationships, there is a fine line between guaranteeing freedom of personal choice and recognizing that the asymmetrical nature of specific relationships calls free choice into question. The following excerpt from a new policy at a very large public university indicates the serious attention that must be given to "consensual" relationships in the workplace.

"Amorous relationships that occur in the context of educational or employment supervision and evaluation present serious concerns about the validity of consent. The element of power implicit in such relationships between a teacher and a student, supervisor and subordinate, or senior and junior colleagues in the same department or unit makes them susceptible to exploitation. . . .

"Relationships between faculty and students are particularly suscepti-ble to exploitation. The respect and trust accorded a member of the faculty by a student, as well as the power exercised by faculty in giving grades or recommendations for further study and future employment, make volun-tary consent by the student suspect.

"Anyone who engages in a sexual relationship with a person over whom he or she has any degree of power or authority within the University structure must understand that the validity of the consent can and may be questioned. In the event of a charge of sexual harassment, the University will give very critical scrutiny to any defense based upon consent when the facts establish that a professional power differential existed within the relationship" (Purdue University, Sexual Harassment Policy 2/15/93).

bility of one romantic relationship in an office leads to the establishment and public emergence of others (Quinn, 1980).

Another potential effect of romance at the workplace is increased dissatisfaction among the workforce. As people begin to feel they are being denied opportunities and resources because of a personal relationship between others (what is sometimes referred to as third party harassment), the communication climate tends to deteriorate, coalitions develop, employees take sides, and some try to enlist the support of others outside the work network. The fear of reprisals also keeps workers from going to their boss to discuss workplace romances. Direct confrontation with a boss who is having an affair is often considered to be professional suicide, hence people feel powerless.

Quinn (1980) provides a vivid example of how organizational romance affects, complicates, and entangles organizational networks.

> As a university administrator in a large non-academic division became involved with a very competent and aggressive secretary, he delegated authority to her and soon she was in conflict with the four men who reported directly to her boss. What had once been known as an exemplary organization was racked with intense hostility. Afraid to approach their boss about the romantic relationship itself, the four department heads tried several times to expose the secretary as incompetent. When the administrator turned a deaf ear to their complaints, they began to spend hours complaining to each other, and then to others outside the division. Decision processes practically ground to a halt and complaints from students increased dramatically. (p. 50)

Consensual sexual activity is clearly problematic for people throughout the networks. There is no set of foolproof guidelines for "coping with Cupid" (Quinn, 1980) but seeing the issue in network rather than individual terms may help organizations find positive and reasonable solutions.

*Sexual harassment.* These issues become complicated even further when we consider that so much communication of a sexual nature is unreciprocated and unwanted by at least one of the people involved. In a government survey conducted in 1981, 42%

of female government workers and 15% of men reported experiencing sexual harassment (Fairhurst, 1986). Intimidation, anger, and frustration are the central elements in harassing relationships. People unwillingly enmeshed in these relationships often show serious effects of stress across domains. Lack of sleep, physical disorders, hyperactivity, and forgetfulness are just some of the symptoms victims experience (Grauerholz & Koralewiski, 1991).

Being involved in an intimidating relationship at work takes its toll in many ways. The employee suffers, the feelings of distress often permeate networks of friends and family who know that "something" is not quite right, and organizational effectiveness is diminished. Organizations are in the early stages of confrontation with these problematic relationships.

Individual responses to sexual harassment vary on several dimensions including assertiveness/passivity, avoidance/confrontation, formal/informal, overt response/ covert response, and direct response/indirect response (Clair, McGoun, & Spirek, 1993). Unfortunately, no particular type of communicative response seems to be more effective than others in stopping the harasser. The psychological and material costs involved in each of these strategies are well documented (MacKinnon, 1979). Livingston (1982) found that in her sample 47% of the women who took formal action felt the situation subsequently improved, 37% thought the situation became worse. Of the women who used assertive objections, 65% believed things got better; 59% who avoided the harasser thought the situation improved; and 43% women thought their most assertive response made no difference, though 54% thought it did. Bingham and Burleson (1989) concentrated on message content and in a study of undergraduate students they found that multifunctional message goals that included "maintaining relational rapport" with the harasser were not any more effective than less sophisticated messages.

Isolated responses to harassment are not effective most of the time. The relationship is so fraught with dangers for the victim and filled with powerful protection for the harasser that there is little motivation for the harassment to stop. Harassment needs to be confronted directly by the larger system and discussed openly in networks across organizations. Institutional support also needs to be given to victims. Class action suits, often designed to alter specific communicative practices within organizations, typically grow out of informal linkages that facilitate shared perceptions and a collective view of experience. When women and men talk to one another outside the official channels, discussing what has heretofore been undiscussible, they may discover their feelings of harassment or discrimination (as in the case of women

*Individual empowerment arises from collective action.*

all receiving lower salaries than their male counterparts) are not indicative of individual capabilities but reflect a systematic bias in the organization. Under these circumstances, harassment will not remain an "open secret that is continually exposed to view yet remains forever unseeable and unsayable" (Cockburn, 1991, p. 170). Individual empowerment arises from collective action.

## RELATIONAL RECIPROCITY

Reciprocity in relationships has several connotations. *Reciprocity* may refer to the degree to which individuals share information and/or disclose personal data and opinions. Reciprocity may also reflect the extent to which one person helps another, returning favors through a network of obligation and gratitude. Albrecht and Adelman (1984) note that the level of communication reciprocity discriminates among networks of mentally disturbed and normal individuals. In the most extreme cases, nonreciprocity may have a spiraling detrimental effect. When people are unable to return the sharing of burdens, resources, and affect that others give them, their networks deteriorate, which leads to continued imbalance (Lipton, Cohen, Fischer, & Katz, 1981).

*Relational reciprocity* can also refer to the degree to which parties share the burdens as well as the advantages of the relationship. Families today are grappling with ways to manage boundaries and balance the ofttimes conflicting demands of the multiple networks in which they are embedded. In contrast to the social industrial policies of Scandinavian and western European na-

## MAKING CONNECTIONS

When Anita Hill testified before Congress that the few close friends she confided in did not advise her to file a formal harassment complaint against Clarence Thomas, her boss and head of the Equal Employment Opportunity Commission (EEOC), she brought public attention to a common communicative practice—that is, the "sequestering" of sexual harassment stories (Clair, 1993).

Organizational storytelling enacts a powerful communicative event. The narrative provides lessons or "morals" for the storyteller and the receiver, facilitates individual and organizational memory of specific content (Martin, Feldman, Hatch, & Sethin, 1983), offers a structured and coherent way in which members internalize prevailing organizational values, plays a key part in members' sense-making activities (Boje, 1991), forms a consensual control mechanism, and serves a political function, usually in the interests of management (Mumby, 1987, 1988). Stories are contextually embedded in the teller's and listeners' networks of experience. Usually brief and fragmented across extended and interrupted discourse, the stories supplement individual memories with institutional memory (Boje, 1991).

Keeping sexual harassment stories within a closely knit network of friends, co-workers, and relatives has several implications for the individual, the network, and the organization. Sequestering stories, isolating them from the mainstream of organizational life, often prevents the wrong being made right, and helps perpetuate the dominance of the harasser specifically and the maintenance of the interests of the dominant group generally. According to Clair (1993), the framing devices of the sequestered narrative may alternatively support or challenge the status quo.

"Framing devices are rhetorical/discursive practices that define or assign interpretation to the social event by the actor or actors" (p. 118). Clair identified several possible framing devices used by women in telling their own stories: (a) accepting the dominant interests as universal (e.g., "It's just best for everyone if I leave"); (b) simple misunderstanding (e.g., "I'm not sure, maybe the man was just flirting with me"); (c) reification ("Men are just that way"); (d) trivialization (e.g., "It was really just a joke"); (e) denotative hesitancy (e.g., "I'm not sure what sexual is but . . ."); (f) private/public expression and private/public domain ("It really is an injustice to his wife"); and (g) minimalization (e.g., "It doesn't happen all the time"). Clair provides several illustrative and fascinating stories. She found that women, although unlikely to frame their stories as simple misunderstandings or reifications—that is, the men may have thought it was lighthearted joking, but the women felt demeaned—did tend to use the other framing devices most often in ways that perpetuated their own victimage. Nonetheless, certain stories were told in ways that transcended the oppression (women labeled their stories as stories of harassment) and as such the sequestered stories were empowering.

tions, where day care and family support is provided by the community and government, individualistic approaches and solutions to work/family issues are more developed in the United States.

Many researchers predict that, as family ties to work organizations increase, the American family will become more rationally organized (Davis, 1982). Feldman (1988), for example, identifies several models of family-work integration that are being pursued by two-parent families. First, the couple can limit the impact of family on work, having few children and subcontracting child-raising activities to day care centers and household help. Second, they can take turns. In this situation, partners trade off career growth opportunities and parenting responsibilities at different points in their lives. Third, the couples can engage in joint ventures where both parents are involved in the same career or same organization. Fourth, they may pursue independent careers to the fullest and cope with the consequences as they arise. Fifth, they can choose to subordinate one career to the other, so that one partner is either out of work or has a much lower investment in the job. Clearly, there is no strategy that is right for all families trying to manage the linkages between work and family lives. Whatever the choice, however, the reciprocal nature of relation ships across domains has reverberations throughout the social matrix. In the long run, family coordination as well as institutional and social policies are necessary to deal effectively with the economic and social needs of families.

Relational reciprocity also refers to the degree to which two people agree upon the type of linkage they share. Network researchers have found that there is considerable variation in self-reported communication behavior and actual communication behavior (Killworth & Bernard, 1976). People higher in the hierarchy, for example, tend to overestimate their downward communication and are more likely to perceive semantic agreement with others than those in less formal hierarchical positions (Contractor, Eisenberg, & Monge, 1992).

The lack of perceptual congruence of network activities has serious implications for organizational life. Imagine the frustration of an engineer who believes she is in close communication

## MAKING CONNECTIONS

People tend to marry people with similar interests, educational levels, and aspirations. Thus it is not surprising that many dual-career couples have jobs in similar industries. In Washington, D.C., the situation is so widespread that as one Washington insider has said, "This town would grind to a halt if the professional lives of women couldn't overlap at all with the professional lives of their husbands" (Barringer, 1992, p. 6).

The large increase of dual-career couples in prominent positions with similar career interests has brought several ethical/communication issues to the public's attention. When lawmakers are married to lobbyists, and health program administrators are married to doctors, issues of personal communication become issues of public concern.

The most pressing and controversial issues revolve around communication—disclosure, confidentiality, conflict of interest, and information sharing. Should a husband or wife be bound to tell of the spouse's connection to the issue at hand? Should husbands and/or wives remove themselves from a specific task? Who decides what is conflict of interest? How much information should the husband and wife share? *New York Times* reporter Felicity Barringer interviewed several Washington couples about the issues. Here are portions of her report.

Harriett N. Babbitt, the wife of former Arizona governor and Secretary of the Interior Bruce Babbitt, who is a lawyer in a Phoenix law firm says, "You absolutely must have disclosure. It's a little like financial disclosure. You say to the world that Susie Q and John Q Public are man and wife. Then people can do what they want with the information."

Ruth Harkin, a lawyer married to Senator Tom Harkin of Iowa, says, "Everyone has their own standards and makes judgment calls." If a legal matter comes up that might overlap with her husband's work on the agriculture, nutrition, and forestry committee (her law firm involves laws and regulations on processed foods), she lets another member of the firm handle it.

Linda Daschle, wife of Senator Tom Daschle from South Dakota, lobbies for airline executives. She reports that she has a written agreement with her employers that she will never lobby her husband.

Gail Wilensky, an administrator of the Health Care Financing Administration, is married to a plastic surgeon who decided not to invest in a radiology lab, in part because such investments might be regulated by his wife. She said, "We decided early on that we had to be very conservative."

Debbie Dingell took herself off the lobbyists' register when she married Representative John Dingell, Michigan Democrat on the House Energy and Commerce Committee, but she is still an executive with General Motors. "I do believe I have to be careful," she said. "I do believe it is wrong for me to lobby. John and I do not talk issues. When certain subjects come up I get up and leave."

These issues cannot easily be resolved. As Ms. Babbitt says, "Life is a series of balancing acts. They are public balancing acts if one of you is involved in public life. That's the reality of both spouses working" (Barringer, 1992, p. 6. Copyright © 1992 by The New York Times Company. Reprinted by permission).

with a project team, yet they believe she is avoiding them. Or consider the potential embarrassment of a person who believes he has a close personal relationship with a co-worker but the other thinks the link is strictly professional. In a study of the semantic and communication networks of employees in three organizations, Contractor et al. (1992) found that, although there wasn't a high correlation between perceived and actual semantic agreement on the meaning of an organizational mission statement, there was a strong relationship between perceived agree-

---

## MAKING CONNECTIONS

Issues of reciprocity and congruence influence even the most conflict-laden relationships. Studies testing Blake and Mouton's (1964) classic model of conflict style consistently find that two relational variables are powerful predictors of which conflict style a person will use—the symmetrical/complementary nature of the relationship and degree of perceptual congruence among the conflicting partners.

Conflict styles are based upon one's position on two fundamental and intersecting continua: (a) the degree of concern for personal goals in a conflict and (b) the importance of your relationship with the other person. If someone scores low on both dimensions, he or she is most likely to use the *avoiding* style. The *forcing* style is used by those who have a high concern for their own personal goals but little concern for the relationship. *Accommodating* styles are exhibited when people have a high concern for relationship and low concern for personal goals. A *collaborating* style represents high concern for both personal goals and the relationship. The *compromising* style is associated with a moderate degree of concern for the relationship and personal goals.

The symmetrical or complementary nature of the relationship has great influence on the type of conflict style one adopts. For example, Putnam and Wilson (1982) indicate that managers tend to use forcing strategies with subordinates, confronting and smoothing styles with superiors, and smoothing and avoiding styles with their peers.

Perceptual congruence and attributions of intent and reciprocity are also associated with conflict style (Putnam & Poole, 1987). When both superior and subordinate concur on the superior's use of forcing strategies, subordinates are more satisfied with work than when they differ on perceptions of the superior's conflict style (Richmond, Davis, Saylor, & McCroskey, 1984). Further, when people use avoiding, forcing, and confronting, they typically report that they perceive the other party is using the same strategy. People in conflict tend to reciprocate the styles of forcing, confronting, smoothing, and compromise. Avoiding tactics usually follow a forcing strategy (Putnam & Poole, 1987).

ment (regardless of whether there was or not) and job satisfaction. In other words, when people thought they were linked to others in the organization through shared interpretations, they were more likely to be satisfied in their job.

RELATIONAL STRENGTH

Relationships will vary in degree of strength. Link strength can be conceptualized in two distinct ways. The most straightforward usage refers to the intensity of the link and is usually based upon frequency of communication, intimacy, or degree of agreement. Strong links represent close, expressive relations and these "primary" ties tend to be in highly segmented clusters. Innovative talk—that is, communication about new and risky ideas—is best encouraged in strong personal ties in an organization (Albrecht & Hall, 1991). Weak instrumental ties (i.e., those arising in the course of performing appointed work roles) tend to be more evenly distributed throughout the system (Blau & Alba, 1982).

Relational strength can also refer to the degree to which a link is connected to other links in the network. From this perspective, a strong link is one that is tightly integrated in the network. Strong ties are easily accessible, highly interconnected, and tend to provide redundant information. Weak ties are those that are loosely connected within a network. Weak ties are less likely to be socially involved with one another than strong ties, and more likely to be connected to some other set of ties not otherwise represented in a person's network. Weak links, particularly those that act as bridges or liaisons between network segments, provide people with access to information and resources beyond those available in their own social circle (Granovetter, 1983). They are more diverse and information rich.

Individuals who are sensitive to the limiting nature of strong ties and the potential "strength of weak ties" often purposefully cultivate diverse relationships. The close circle of advisers surrounding leaders tend to give the same advice not necessarily because they are ambitious sycophants but because they share the same worldview—they share the same types of experiences, they talk to the same types of people, they experience the world in the same way. Arthur Schlesinger's account of Franklin Delano Roosevelt as a "consummate networker" describes a leader who is cognizant of the truth behind the saying, "Men who know the same things are not profitable company for one another."

> The first task of an executive, as Roosevelt saw it, was to guarantee himself an effective flow of information and ideas. Roosevelt's persistent effort, therefore, was to check and balance information acquired through official channels by information acquired through a myriad of private, informal, and unorthodox channels and espionage networks. At times, he seemed almost to pit his personal sources against his public sources. (cited in Deal & Kennedy, 1982, pp. 86, 87)

When people are unable to bring outsiders into highly interconnected network deliberations, they often try to simulate the advantage of weak ties by appointing people special roles such as "devil's advocate" (Janis, 1989). The activities associated with such roles include "seeing the world in a different way," not accepting the fundamental premises upon which arguments are built in the group, and voicing concerns and reservations. In other words, the person is expected to act as an outsider, to play the role of someone who hasn't been socialized into the group's culture, that is, a person with little need to feel included in the group. Although described in terms of individuals, the patterned set of behavioral expectations that constitute a "role" are essentially descriptions of network relationships.

## RELATIONAL ROLES

The term *role* has been used in several ways. First, it can delineate a specific interpersonal relationship such as student/teacher, employer/employee, and parent/child. Second, network roles indicate a person's location within the social system. Third, roles can be used to describe a set of expectations about activities associated with a particular position. Wofford, Gerloff, and Cummins (1979) distinguish three types of role expectations. The *perceived role* is the set of behaviors that the occupant of the position believes he or she should perform. The *expected role* is the set of behaviors that others believe he or she should perform. An *enacted role* is the actual set of behaviors performed.

Role expectations may be position bound and prescribed or emergent. Positional role expectations encompass "designated behaviors and obligatory relations incumbent upon the people in positions. The positions and the roles are formally defined in the organization and exist independently of the individuals who fill them" (Monge & Eisenberg, 1987, p. 305). Emergent role expectations arise out of interaction across networks. The communication and activities that define the relationship do not necessarily coincide with prescribed roles.

*Role ambiguity* is the degree of uncertainty an individual has concerning what behavior is appropriate in a particular role. Role ambiguity has traditionally been associated with negative consequences such as turnover, dissatisfaction, anxiety, and low performance (Miller, Ellis, Zook, & Lyles, 1990). Effective socialization practices are considered to be those that prepare the employee to perform his or her roles adequately. Members of the employee's network clarify role expectations and provide role models (Jablin, 1987). Like message ambiguity, however, role ambiguity may also serve positive functions for the individual as well as the organization. Ambiguity provides workers with latitude and freedom to make their jobs more comfortable, to be more effective, to do the things they like to do, to do what they think should be done, and to establish relationships they feel would be beneficial. Role ambiguity also provides flexibility, allowing the organization to be more creative and responsive to change (Martin & Meyerson, 1988).

In contrast to role ambiguity, which leaves space for the individual to act more autonomously, role conflict—"the simultaneous occurrence of two or more competing role expectations" (Katz & Kahn, 1966)—often creates such a tightly constrained system that the individual feels powerless in several relationships. Role conflict can occur across relationships within an organization. For example, if you are a residence hall counselor and a student, you may find yourself unable to fulfill obligations from each role. What do you do when your floor residents expect you to attend the big holiday party being held at the only time your political science group can meet to finish the final class project? Role conflict can occur across contexts; the behavioral expectations of being a parent may conflict with the expectations of being a high school principal. For example, do you attend your school's banquet honoring the football team's state championship or do you attend your own child's soccer match?

Nowhere are permeable boundaries more apparent than when we consider role expectations and the potential for conflict in those situations in which workers are employed in jobs typically associated with the other gender (e.g., male nurse, female fire fighter, male day care worker, female doctor; see Wood & Conrad, 1983). Women in traditionally male roles often threaten male dominance; men in women's roles create anomalies and paradox.

Individuals are likely to experience conflict based on the clash between what is expected on the job and societal sex role expectations that "spill over" into the workplace (Gutek & Morasch, 1982). The harassment female construction workers face has little, if anything, to do with their actions on the job; rather, their work roles are undermined by societal sex roles in which women are considered first and foremost sexual beings, nurturing and dependent (Fairhurst, 1986; Hearn & Parkin, 1987). Men who do "female" work may be less likely to face overt hostility on the job

*Communication may both resolve and perpetuate organizational paradoxes.*

(they are not directly assaulting the power structure), but stress and strain often come from parents, especially fathers, and "first contact and superficial relationships" (Fairhurst, 1986, p. 88).

Communication may both resolve and perpetuate the paradoxes resulting from the importation and overlap of role expectations across networks. The "male nurse" who redefines his job as "doctor's aide" may avoid the female (and hence contradictory) connotations associated with the nursing profession but he also reinforces the linkage of nursing with feminine abilities. The "female doctor" who publicly objects to the adjective *female* being used because it differentiates her from "regular doctors" at-

## MAKING CONNECTIONS

Organizational discourse structures the identities of individuals as they confront day-to-day tasks (Mumby & Stohl, 1991). Certain possibilities, certain relations, are systematically included while others are just as systematically excluded. The following excerpt from a male's description of his experience as a newly employed secretary in a large Boston bank (Finder, 1987, p. 68) indicates how organizational identities and power relationships do not arise solely from experiences within the organizations but are woven from the fabric of social experience. Note how the conversations with the male secretary were addressed along gender lines; that is, he was addressed as a male rather than a secretary. The conversations between the men enacted a relationship of equals; the manager explicitly avoided interacting with the male as a secretary. For the secretaries, the incongruity was dealt with in a manner that reinforced his "superior" position, affirmed the power structure of the organization, and minimized the chance that he actually could be a male secretary. By denying him the opportunity to become a "real" secretary, occupational segregation—that is, the "pink collar ghetto"—was reaffirmed. Despite the chance for change, business would continue as usual.

"An executive from another floor came up to my desk and said, 'The girl's on leave?' He thought I was a management trainee helping out the beleaguered staff. I told him that, no, I was the new secretary, but he just laughed, certain I was kidding.

"The other secretaries on the floor were plainly disbelieving. 'So what do you do?' asked one of the older women, after a coffee break one day.

"What do you mean, I said, I'm a secretary.

"She laughed, 'Are you a student?'

"No, actually I graduated.

" 'Come on,' she said. 'This stuff is too boring for you.' She paused, then added, 'Honey, I've got to do this. You don't have to. You'll be moving into management. Guys aren't secretaries. . . .'

"I was an anomalous creature to just about everyone in the office, a man who wasn't in management, and a secretary who wasn't a woman. No one ever asked me to get coffee, but they'd ask me to lift heavy sacks of mail or cartons of loan forms or try to fix the copying machine. My boss refused to give me anything to type. He would go out of his way to take something he needed typed to a secretary on another part of the floor.

"With female secretaries, he dealt in a crisp, professional manner, softened with banter and jokes. With me, he pretended that I wasn't really a secretary at all. It wasn't as if he ignored me; every half hour or so he would emerge from his office to talk sports with me and exchange dirty jokes. Both of us effectively ignored two facts: that my job was to do his clerical work and that he couldn't accept that. 'Hey Joe,' he would announce coming out of his office and dumping a wad of paper into a trash can. 'You catch those Celtics last night?'

" 'No, I'd say. How they'd do?' " (Copyright © 1987 by The New York Times Company. Reprinted by permission).

tempts to unravel the relational paradox through communication but may perpetuate the distinction by calling attention to the difference between her and other doctors. Nonetheless, the increasing presence of males and females in occupational networks that have traditionally been associated with a single sex has begun to engender changes in the taken-for-granted assumptions about what type of relationship constitutes a particular role. As personal networks become more diverse and linkages less stereotypical, organizational communication will change.

## ❑ Final Connections

Relationships bring organizations to life. They constitute the design and rich patterns of collective experience. *Relationships are unique but only make sense in the context of other relationships.* Within our networks, we find our selves. *Relationships facilitate and hinder our individuality.* Messages cannot be understood independent of relationships; relationships cannot exist without messages.

In this chapter, we have focused on the interpersonal dynamics of organizational relationships and explored five characteristics of relationships that strongly influence the manner in which organizing takes place: orientation, multiplexity, symmetry, reciprocity, and strength. The complexity and vigor of organizational relationships constitute a potential and powerful dynamic of change.

# PART III

# Linking Communication
# and Organization

# Hierarchy

*The previous chapters highlighted the fundamental units of organizations. In this chapter, we enrich our understanding of organizational communication by examining the ways messages and relationships are interwoven into one of the most pervasive network patterns—hierarchy.*

Hierarchies are central features in images of both work and home lives. A recent study of American character, values, and traditions, *Habits of the Heart* (Bellah, Madsen, Sullivan, Swidler, & Tipton, 1985), suggests that the American dream defines success as advancing up the hierarchy, while another best-seller discusses Americans' *Fear of Falling* (Ehrenrich, 1989). Even cartoons satirize the importance of hierarchy in our lives. For example, a cartoon by Joseph Mirachi in *The New Yorker* (1986) portrays an innocent child looking up expectantly at his father and asking, "Say, Pop, where do you stand in the pecking order?"

Despite its dominance as the paradigmatic organizational structure, the idea of hierarchy is often regarded as inconsistent with the American ideal of equality. In some cases, we deny the existence of hierarchy ("We are all equals here") and in other situations we view its presence with great suspicion ("Who's really in charge here?"). A democratic vision, coupled with the practical pressures of a highly interconnected information society, have strengthened the impetus to explore alternative ways of organizing. Theorists are proposing new forms of organizations that would be non-hierarchical, open, and sensitive to the constituents' interests (e.g., Acker, 1990; Deetz, 1992; Gottfried & Weiss, 1994). Profit and non-profit organizations are attempting to create more responsive and flexible organizations by redesigning organizational hierarchies. Pyramids are getting flatter, corporate layers are getting thinner, and social networks are getting wider. Extensive computer networks are heralded as the technology that will bring an end to the old hierarchical structures of large multinational corporations (Taylor & Van Every, 1993).

Efforts to invigorate participatory processes and democratize the workplace will be discussed in the next chapter. Before we are able to understand these alternatives, however, it is important to consider hierarchy as a prototypical relational pattern. Hierarchical networks are the standards by which alternative ways of organizing are compared and contrasted. Furthermore, although the formalized, highly stratified task hierarchies of the past are being modified, hierarchical arrangements are still commonplace in most social contexts.

In this chapter, we shall see that hierarchies are created, re-created, sustained, and changed through communicative practices. Consider, for a moment, your involvement in even just a few groups (e.g., family, sorority, softball team, honors class, poker group, student government). In almost all cases, a hierarchy does exist and you have a specific place in it. Often, our positions are highly consistent across situations. Both our strong and weak ties include links to other individuals of elevated status. We are embedded in clusters of high-achieving and resource-rich relations and our attitudes and perceptions are closely aligned with those individuals. We know how to dress, what to discuss, and how to discuss it. We can "take charge" and align ourselves with powerful others.

Just as the privileges of high status transcend contexts, the disadvantages of low hierarchical positions are often difficult to overcome. Many people enter the workplace unaware and/or uncertain of how to communicate in ways that will help them move up the established hierarchy. If one has never been a central figure in a network and/or has never been accorded the advantages and opportunities of rank, the subtle communicative activities of improving status are difficult to learn without some guidance from mentors, supportive colleagues, or other interested parties. This chapter explores the nature of hierarchical relationships in organizations as they are embedded in overlapping networks.

---

### MAKING CONNECTIONS

When experiences both in and out of the workplace continually reinforce each other, people begin to see the world through the same lenses. The clustering of people from similar hierarchical and occupational levels, but not necessarily similar organizations, is conspicuous in the neighborhoods we live in, the recreational activities we choose, the schools our children attend, the volunteer organizations we participate in, and the social clubs we join. Because proximity is the best predictor of communicative practices, it is not surprising that managers who live and play next to other managers talk to and persuade one another, and hourly workers who live and play side by side interact with and influence one another.

But the implications of such clustering go beyond simple frequency of interaction. Cost alone may ensure that working-class people are not playing on the same golf courses as CEOs or sending their children to the same private schools, but the social dynamics that separate people across the hierarchy go beyond economic opportunity.

There is strong evidence to suggest that hierarchical level is associated with the types of magazines people read, the movies they choose, the television programs they watch, their topics of conversation, and so forth. Upwardly mobile young executives learn very quickly that they are expected to sprinkle conversations with facts culled from *Fortune* magazine and the *Wall Street Journal*, they are not expected to read or discuss the latest issue of *The National Inquirer*. Secretaries are not expected to discuss the latest debate in the *Times Literary Supplement*. Research has shown that differential exposure to mass media has significant effects on people's attitudes, values, and beliefs (Hirschman, 1981). By reading, watching, and discussing only those viewpoints associated with particular hierarchical levels and validated in the "appropriate" media, individuals become enmeshed in a self-perpetuated interpretive framework, continually reinforcing a particular worldview.

Three major themes are developed: (a) Hierarchical networks are sustained through communication practices; (b) despite the possibility for alternative ways of organizing, hierarchical networks are pervasive; and (c) hierarchies serve multiple functions.

## ❏ The Nature of Hierarchical Relationships

Most simply, a hierarchy is a *relational matrix of status or authority ranking one set of linkages above another in a series.* In organized social systems, *hierarchies are constituted by networks of graded relationships that both pattern and are patterned by communication systems.* Formal hierarchies represent an enactment of "stipulated vertical [communication] channels" (McPhee, 1986) and also reflect emergent communication patterns. As graphically depicted in organizational charts, formal hierarchies are pyramidal structures with one figure at the top and successively more numerous but less powerful subordinates below in one horizontal level after another. Informal hierarchies, less constrained by the official organizational design, exist alongside the official hierarchy.

---

**MAKING CONNECTIONS**

While certainly not creating the notion of hierarchy, German sociologist *Max Weber* played a key role in formalizing the place of hierarchy in organizational theory. Hierarchy is a critical element in his model of bureaucracy. Writing in the early decades of this century, Weber was seeking an alternative to forms of organization in which favoritism was often rampant, rules were often designed to serve individual rather than organizational needs, and powerful individuals, typically a foreman or general manager, wielded power in often arbitrary and capricious ways. Weber sought to develop an organizational design that would eliminate all the extraorganizational forces acting on organizational members, thus creating an impersonal and rational system, a human system offering the same precision, speed, and efficiency as the machines of the new industrial age. While recognizing that actual bureaucracies would deviate from his ideal model, Weber did not pursue the nature of these differences.

*(continued)*

Hierarchies develop through collaborative relationships. Cultural values, demographic characteristics, personal attributes, social attributes, and/or competency levels contribute to one's place in any given hierarchy as does one's position in other hierarchies. Each position serves to constrain or empower the how, what, when, where, and with whom you can and will communicate. Our understanding of hierarchies therefore cannot be tied to a specific location. Each can only be understood as part of the comprehensive field of social interaction, each network of relationships is implicated in the other.

To illustrate, imagine the son of the chairman of the board as he enters his father's organization. We would expect him to be more highly placed in both formal and informal hierarchies than other new recruits with the same entry-level position. First, he is male, and often gender is an important aspect of hierarchical placement. Second, he is probably a member of the dominant socioeconomic, religious, and cultural groups in the system and so is already familiar with the expectations, standards, behaviors, and norms associated with upper ranks. Third, he is probably being paid a salary, rather than an hourly wage, a common financial discriminator among hierarchical levels. Fourth, chances are he knows and talks socially with many of the key actors in the dominant coalitions of the corporation. Fifth, many will believe that a close connection with the son will help their own

Hallmarks of Weber's new "bureaucratic model" of organizing include *division of labor* based on specialization, selection and promotion based on *technical qualifications*, operations governed by *rules and their consistent application*, specification of the *rights and responsibilities* of each office, and, holding it all together, a clear *hierarchical system of authority*. In a bureaucracy, Weber (1947) wrote, "The organization of offices follows the principle of hierarchy; that is, each lower office is under control and supervision of a higher one" (p. 89). The official hierarchy, the organizational chart as it is often called, thus becomes the blueprint for distributing authority throughout the organization. The clear distribution of authority throughout the hierarchy, Weber argued, would make for a highly efficient system of decision making. In such a bureaucracy, individuals' actions would be mechanistically derived from the formal rules, thus ensuring continuity and predictability in organizational life.

## MAKING CONNECTIONS

Our hierarchical position outside a particular organizational context has a strong impact on our position within an organization. The expression "the rich get richer" not only applies to the acquisition of money, it often relates to the acquisition of knowledge, resources, and important network connections. For example, institutional ties play an important role in career development and the ability to move up the corporate ladder. The name of the university from which you graduate sends a powerful message to employees about your connections, your competencies, and your place in several hierarchies. Significantly, people who attend elite universities tend to come from families who are already a part of the economic elite; the connections made at school reinforce the connections found at home.

The degree to which college affiliation affects your future, however, varies from country to country. In the United States, for example, job performance, reputation, and unique skills mediate the effect of institutional ties. Most career options are open to people who graduated from less prestigious schools. Alternatively, in countries like France and Japan, institutional affiliation is an extremely important factor in where you fit in society, in your position in social, organizational, and interorganizational hierarchies.

For example, when a Japanese business person asks another what school he or she attended, the question does not merely constitute polite small talk. Rather, the answer provides an overall assessment of the person's present and future career, his or her position in the organizational hierarchy, and in society in general. It is common knowledge in Japanese culture that if a student does not get into Todai (Tokyo University) his or her chances of joining top-ranking companies and/or ministries are exceedingly small. Those who succeed in getting into Tokyo University have entrance into an elite and privileged network. The strong bond that develops among graduates from these prestigious schools (the cliques are called *gakubatsu*) "encourages a web of obligations based on favors traded" (DeMente, 1981, p. 34). Thus the graduates of elite institutions are strongly advantaged when it comes to business deals and decisions.

In France, elitism is preserved through the *grandes écoles*. But unlike Japan, where graduates from the top university get the top jobs across industries, in France the advantage of a particular university over another is field dependent. Government or service officials usually attend the École Nationale d'Administration, production management and engineers come from École Polytechnique and École Centrale. Here again, the outstanding education received by students at the grandes ecoles plays only one part in the powerful influence they yield in governmental and business spheres. Rather, hierarchical position is derived from "the web of networking among alumni that creates a sort of club of carefully scrutinized and limited membership among the ruling business and government elite" (Victor, 1992, p. 88). For international business and governmental officials, it is important to realize the "powerful" and critical message that is sent when they align themselves with alumni of these prestigious universities.

career. Therefore he will probably be invited places other new employees are not, and told important and strategic information, far beyond what is usually shared or discussed with a new recruit. Overall, he becomes more knowledgeable, reinforcing others' beliefs that he is "in the know," and thus strengthening his high hierarchical placement across a series of networks.

Now consider what happens if he joins a company-sponsored support group for dual-career families. Although the group exists primarily for social support and advice and is not hierarchically structured, other group members would be aware of his connection to the president. Therefore, even though the two systems are supposed to be unrelated, other employees would likely monitor their interactions in his presence, censoring some sentiments and being sure to express others. In other words, they would enact communication rules brought over from the formal hierarchical system, thus importing and re-creating a previously established hierarchical network.

---

### MAKING CONNECTIONS

Organizational researchers have long recognized that the power of individuals is largely a function of the extent to which they have access to information, persons, and resources (Mechanic, 1962). Employees who are enmeshed in information- and resource-rich networks can build coalitions with powerful supporters and are likely to be more successful.

The difficulties many women and minorities have when they enter the workplace can be explained in large part by the social matrix within which they are embedded. The interpersonal communication differences among men, women, and minorities play only a small part in understanding why women and minorities have been unable to move up the hierarchy at the same rate as their white male counterparts. The unequivocal conclusion of dozens of studies is that gender and racially segregated interaction patterns deny women and minorities access to the information, resource allocation, and support that would aid their mobility and success in the organization.

For example, Brass (1985) studied the interaction patterns of men and women in an organization and the relationship of these patterns to (a) perceptions of influence and (b) promotions to supervisory positions.

The results indicate that an individual's position in the work flow and interaction networks relates strongly to measures of influence. Although women were rated as less influential than men, both gender groups had

*(continued)*

As the example of the chairman's son illustrates, *communication is simultaneously the source, the process, and the outcome of hierarchical position.* People who occupy high positions in a hierarchy tend to be those who have larger networks, are more central in the communication flow, and are more interconnected with others of high status. Contrary to popular belief, it is not necessarily "lonely at the top." Bell, Roloff, VanCamp, and Karsol (1990), for example, found that hierarchical rank was associated neither with loneliness nor scarcity of friends or partner. High-level employees tend to work longer hours, but the additional re-

---

similar performance evaluations. Women who were perceived as less influential were not well integrated into men's networks. Promotions were also significantly related to centrality in departmental, men's, and the dominant coalitions' interaction networks. The lack of integration in these critical networks (women were more integrated into other organizational networks) is particularly meaningful given that over 45% of the employees in the organization studied were women. Therefore it is not that there were fewer women in general but that women, despite their numbers, tended to cluster together and were out of the "power loops."

Why have women been excluded, or why do they exclude themselves, from male networks? The answers may range from an emphasis on women's naïveté to intentional discriminatory practices on the part of the power holders. Can you think of other possibilities?

1. Women are not aware of the importance of being enmeshed in richly textured networks. They have had little experience doing it, so they are not as adept as men in "networking" skills.

2. It is easier to communicate with people similar to oneself in terms of experience, values, and attitudes, thus women do not seek out men and men do not seek out women.

3. Women recognize the inherent danger in socializing with men—from rumors of their looseness to the possibility of sexual assault. Hence women may avoid all contact with males outside contexts directly related to a specific work task. Men may feel the same discomfort and avoid women.

4. Segregation is a rational response of organizations to limit uncertainty.

5. Men purposefully prevent women from entering their networks. The segregation can be seen in the formal exclusionary practices of private clubs as well as in the informal actions in social networks. Furthermore, men who are cognizant of and disagree with these social practices find it very difficult to take issue directly and personally with such activities. Thus they do not confront the issue and do not help instigate change.

sources, status, and flexibility available to them compensate for the lack of time. They are just as likely to maintain friendships as employees at lower levels although the friendships are more likely to have developed from work connections. Individuals with low hierarchical rank often tend to have fewer resources available, and their work networks are limited and homogeneous. Is it communication that causes/affects hierarchical placement or is it hierarchical placement that causes/affects communication? The answer, clearly, is both.

## ❑ The Persuasiveness of Hierarchy

Hierarchy's presence is so pervasive in society, it may seem impossible to move beyond it in formally organized contexts. Michels's (1962) famous "iron law of oligarchy" specifies that organizations move in a unidirectional path toward increasing bureaucratization. Burke (1969) argues that hierarchy is a defining characteristic of humans. More studies deal with "superior/ subordinate" communication (a complementary relationship that presumes the existence of hierarchy) than any other relational context in organizations (Stohl & Redding, 1987). Some suggest that the hierarchical network pattern that dominates the modern American complex organization is a result of men's earlier socialization experiences.

> It is the way most armies are organized—platoon, company, battalion, brigade, division, corps, army—and if you want to make a million men advance or retreat at a few hours' notice it is hard to think of a better system. I suspect that it is service with the army in two world wars that has imprinted this organizational pattern on so many managerial minds with the modern corporations, even though making a million men advance or retreat at a few hours' notice is a problem they can only encounter very infrequently. (Schrank, 1978, p. 3)

Scholars within the *critical tradition* argue that we have been socialized to see hierarchy as the natural state of affairs because historically it has served and continues to serve the purposes of the ruling class (Deetz, 1992). Hierarchy keeps challenges away from the authoritarian structure. Tompkins (1987) reminds us that "the essence of Weber's bureaucracy is, if reduced to a word, hierarchy" (p. 81). Cheney (1991) notes: "To open up channels of communication to all levels is to invite challenges to institutional authority and hierarchical identity" (p. 175). Consequently, even when people are given the opportunity to behave in a non-hierarchical

---

### MAKING CONNECTIONS

The higher individuals' positions in an hierarchy, the more likely they will have opportunities to enhance their chances of moving or remaining on top and to decrease the likelihood of those below them taking their place. For example, a University of Michigan business professor runs a five-week course that costs companies up to $45,000 for each person they enroll. The point of the intensive program is to teach corporate executives the communication skills and analytic approaches that will help them become better managers in the international system. Activities include communication exercises and discussions that highlight cultural differences. For example, after going through several group discussions, participants begin to recognize that Americans like to take control of meetings and high-status Japanese would prefer to listen. Two weeks of travel in Brazil, India, and China help executives learn specifics about industrial practices while forcing them to deal directly with cultural differences. The executives also spend a weekend on Hurricane Island in Maine with the Outward Bound School, completing group activities such as mountain rappelling, caving, and raft racing with their international colleagues. Multicultural teams prepare oral, written, and video reports sharing their ideas about management.

The sponsors of this program claim that the executives learn to interact in a more flexible manner and understand there is more than one way to approach and solve problems. But as they themselves admit, perhaps the most significant and long-term effect of this program is the development of relationships with one another.

These high-ranking executives become friends, forming a supportive network that remains long after the specific content of the course has faded from memory. The hilarious evenings spent performing skits and playing charades as well as the participation in one another's cultural rituals encourage rich multiplex linkages. These connections are very useful once the executives leave the course. Each executive now has access to information and resources that are denied others (not through any lack of competence on the others part but merely from lack of opportunity to forge these alliances). Each is able to perform his executive functions in ways that others cannot match. Each now has an enriched personal network that is very useful for the organization. Already highly positioned in the hierarchy, they are likely to go even higher (J. Main, 1989, *Fortune* © 1989 Time Inc. All rights reserved).

manner, it often is difficult to do so because they have neither the experience nor the appropriate communicative models.

Hierarchy may also develop as a result of outside tensions and the inevitable pressures of an interconnected world. For example, many groups that are committed to democratic and feminist principles find they must create a multileveled bureaucratic structure to procure grants for undertaking community projects and maintain funding support from outside agencies (Adams, 1983; Ferree, 1987). Ironically, the advisory panels, policy-making boards, and specialized interest groups that arise to deal with these agencies may unintentionally segment internal networks and mirror the hierarchies that are antithetical to the values of the organizations.

## ❏ Recognizing and Enacting Hierarchies

Whatever the reasons for their development, hierarchical patterns are so pervasive in social systems it is essential that individuals learn how to recognize and interpret them. Being knowledgeable about hierarchical structures and cognizant of the obtrusive as well as unobtrusive workings of hierarchical networks empowers individuals in overt as well as subtle ways. Most individuals prefer to be seen as competent members of the organizations to which they belong, and if they do violate the existing hierarchical patterns,

*Hierarchy is apparent in the communicative practices that constitute organizational networks.*

they want to do so as a matter of choice rather than ignorance. Furthermore, understanding hierarchical networks helps individuals to make sense of the environment, reduce uncertainty, and develop strategies for advancing their own careers. Finally, if individuals want to change systems, they must understand how their own actions, as well as others', produce and reproduce hierarchical systems.

How then do we recognize and enact multiple hierarchies? Some organizations (e.g., many of the new American-Japanese

joint ventures and new sociotechnical system designs) are especially anxious to eliminate obvious signs of hierarchical division
so as to communicate a desire and commitment to a "workplace
democracy" and "individual creativity." These organizations often abandon the traditional trappings and obvious perquisites of
hierarchy such as reserved parking places for executives, dress
differences, or the use of titles. Nonetheless, employee experience in such organizations often suggests that the elimination of
hierarchical divisions is more apparent than real. If one were to
observe closely, they argue, signs of hierarchy would become
apparent in the communicative practices that constitute organizational networks.

---

### MAKING CONNECTIONS

Although there is some evidence to suggest that American baby boomers are not nearly as concerned with moving up the hierarchy as their older
counterparts (Hall & Richter, 1990), American workers still spend more
than "$150 million annually in an attempt to appear more powerful and
polished." Charging as much as $500 per session, consultants across the
United States teach ambitious men and women how to package themselves
so as to climb the ever-narrowing corporate ladder.

In 1990 the *Directory of Personal Image Consultants* listed over 350 registered professionals. Daylong seminars with titles like "Marketing Yourself
in Tough Times" focus on image making. Clients learn how to become more
visible in powerful networks as well as how to change their image if they
are not being perceived as they would like to be.

Many of the lessons taught at these seminars have little, if anything, to
do with actual job skills. For example, Camille Lavington, a New York
image consultant, told a *New York Times* reporter that Lesson 1 is "always
share a meal to develop rapport with your business associates." Moving
beyond basic "how to dress for success" tips, these consultants teach clients
the proper way to hold a fork and knife, the etiquette of ordering in a fancy
restaurant, and the appropriate way to respond to an invitation. In other
words, the consultants teach people the social and presentational skills that
are second nature to those who are born into the upper echelons of society.
Reinforcing the idea that hierarchy is inevitable and one must learn how
to package oneself to fit in, the consultants present a view of organizational
life that is not much different than that of the organizations of the 1950s.
In the words of consultant Lavington: "There are only two kinds of people
in the business world: eagles and mosquitoes. You either soar with the
eagles or you swarm with the mosquitoes" (Better, 1991, p. 29. Copyright
© 1991 by The New York Times Company. Reprinted by permission).

HIERARCHICAL DISCOURSE

The discursive practices of hierarchy are often learned outside a particular organizational context. From our earliest experiences in family and school, we are socialized to communicate in ways that recreate hierarchical divisions. Mitchell's (1979) description of bureaucratic discourse is as applicable to communication between student and principal as to worker and manager.

---

## MAKING CONNECTIONS

Understanding the meaning behind titles is an important organizational skill. For example, whether you are called a "managing director" or "executive" sends a message to others (traditionally, managers are not nearly as important as executives). Yet, as with most language, the meanings of titles are fluid and differentially interpreted by diverse networks. Furthermore, the era of globalization and international networking has radically changed the terms upon which hierarchical positions are communicated. In England, for example, the term *chairman* or *chairwoman* indicates the person is actively involved in the daily management of the company, whereas in the United States, if a person is referred to as the "chairman" or "chairwoman" of a large company, most people assume he or she is the head of the board of directors, removed from active management, and hence less influential or involved in the everyday affairs of the organization.

The close association between titles and power underlies the moral of a widely told story at W. L. Gore & Associates, a company well known as the manufacturer of Gore-Tex, which claims to have created a conscious alternative to top-down hierarchical organizations. At Gore, the networking management structure is called a "lattice organization." The more than 2,000 associates (not employees) are grouped around projects and the projects are undertaken on the basis of commitment with one's sponsor (not boss). Michael Pacanowsky (1988), a communication scholar who has worked as a consultant for Gore, tells the story of a Gore associate, Sarah Clifton, who was a member of a women's professional club.

"As the other women had business cards to distribute indicating their lofty positions, and all she had was a card that said Associate, she felt a certain discomfort. Her sponsor at the time, Peter Cooper, told her she should just make up a lofty title for herself, that associates need to be 'associates' on the inside but that they could take whatever titles they wanted in dealing with people on the outside. So as a joke, Peter had some business cards made up for Sarah that identified her as "Sara Clifton, W. L. Gore & Associates, Supreme commander" (p. 373).

It is a mistake to think that the language of the bureaucrats is merely an ignorant, garbled jargon. They may not always know what they are doing, but what they are doing is not haphazard. It works, too. For example, messages in the passive voice, ("It has been brought to the attention of this office," rather than "I see that") or laden with legalistic terminology ("You are hereby notified that . . .") depersonalize and abstract interactions, making it clear that "one of the rulers is addressing one of the ruled." (Mitchell, 1979, p. 34)

Hierarchical differentiation is also achieved through interaction management. According to many communication scholars, interaction management is a significant component of all types of relationships (Eisenberg et al., 1983; Wiemann, 1977). Simple things like who controls the topic of conversation, who interrupts whom, and floor time allocation (who spends the greatest amount of time speaking) reproduce hierarchical relationships within and between network clusters. In many cultures, the "time" of some individuals is more valuable than that of others. It seems natural that doctors keep patients waiting, managers put subordinates on hold, and parents make children "be patient." Even the right to correct another's mistakes is vested in hierarchy. A colleague named Susan was called Diane during her entire job interview with the president of a college. Not once during this 45-minute interaction did she correct him, knowing that to do so would cause embarrassment and perhaps lessen her chances of getting the job.

Generally the absence of specific sanctioning communication when an interaction norm has been violated is an indicator of the relatively high status of the violator within a network. Individuals with high degrees of competence and hierarchical stature usually have earned "idiosyncrasy credits" allowing them not to follow all the rules that others must (Hollander, 1958). The aside comment, once overheard following a bad joke, "You don't have to laugh, you are the Dean," spoke more truth than the light-hearted teasing suggested. We must be careful, however, not to judge too quickly. Newcomers and those already labeled as "lost causes" or "deviants" within a network may also be seen to transgress appropriate standards without punishment.

Taking note of interaction sequences is particularly helpful in identifying the ways in which hierarchy is discursively produced. Communication scholars Rogers and Farace (1975) have developed procedures for identifying message exchange patterns that represent different types of *relational control*. Complementary interactions consist of one person's attempt to restrict the options of the other, and the other person willingly relinquishing his or her options. In symmetrical exchanges, interac-

---

### MAKING CONNECTIONS

In the article excerpted below, a female secretary describes her perceptions of a "caste system" in American universities. Her analysis points out (a) some ways in which hierarchy is communicatively produced and sustained within networks and (b) how the gender-based division of labor that has typically been found in the domestic sphere is reproduced within the workplace.

Women's work has traditionally been invisible, whereas men's work is obtrusive, considered more important, and valued more highly. Gillette's analysis demonstrates how these patriarchal/hierarchical relations *structurally* exist and persist in the institutions and social practices of our society. Interpersonal communication cannot be explained solely by the intentions, good or bad, of individual men or women.

"A key feature of any caste system is that those above behave as if those below were non-people. In academe, secretaries are thought not to share the same level of humanity as faculty members. For example, for a time my desk was in the foyer leading to faculty offices. The faculty would discuss private details of their students' performance and qualifications, or say what they thought of their colleagues, within my hearing. It was as though they assumed I could not comprehend their conversation, or perhaps they thought of me as a piece of furniture. Whatever the case, I was treated as a non-person, forced to feign deafness to protect their indiscretions.

"When I had a private office that I could lock, I was not allowed to decorate it according to my taste. My supervisor entered [broke into?] my locked office when I was absent and rearranged it herself. Needless to say, she would never have rearranged the office of a real person, a faculty member . . .

"A secretary is often the recipient of unwanted confidences from faculty members, who dump their worries about their families and money and cars on her. If the secretary brings up a problem of her own, however, the conversation abruptly ends. The caste system is a one-way street, requiring that the faculty members receive, not dispense, sympathy and concern" (Gillette, 1987, p. 96).

tants are communicating as equals: competitively, submissively, or neutrally. People assert their status by using more "one-ups" and fewer "one-downs" or "one-acrosses." Networks in which there is a high frequency of one-across symmetrical verbal exchanges tend to be less hierarchically structured in others ways as well (Fairhurst, Rogers, & Sarr, 1987).

Just as verbal interaction reflects hierarchical relationships, non-verbal messages also produce and index relative status. Many of the classic organizational "status symbols" such as having an executive desk, a personal secretary, use of a company car, or a large corner office are frequently intended to validate publicly the formal hierarchy. It is important to remember, however, that the meanings of these symbols vary according to the networks in which one is enmeshed. In China, for example, room layouts that are not in harmony with nature have bad *feng shui* and, no matter how large or how many windows it contains, the room will be avoided by all (Adler, 1991).

In Western culture, increasing amounts of private space or "territory" connote increasing power and status. Typically, people of higher status "mark their territory" with personal items such as photos or mementos, while in many organizations low-level employees are not even allowed to have "personal items" at their desks or workstations. The permeability of personal space is also linked to hierarchy, with individuals of higher status being more free to enter the space of a lower ranked individual (whether a child's bedroom, a student's locker, or an employee's work area).

## ❏ Hierarchies Serve Multiple Functions

Although hierarchies tend to marginalize specific groups and are often blamed for organizational ills (e.g., "There's too much red tape." "I can't seem to talk to whoever is really in charge here."), formal hierarchical relationships are adopted, at least in theory, to enhance administrative efficiency. In the ideal system, each successive layer of the hierarchy supervises the work of those below and transmits policy and plans downward and intelligence and inquiries upward (Katz & Kahn, 1966). Individuals build their careers and serve the company by doggedly climbing the corporate ladder.

Two terms commonly associated with the ideal "bureaucratic model" are *chain of command* and *span of control*. Each term designates structurally prescribed features of networks designed to keep the activities of the system maximally coordinated and productive. The *chain of command* refers to the formalized prescription of responsibility, describing appropriate patterns of communication activity within a bounded system. Traditionally, a hierarchy is designed so that each individual is directly responsible to one immediate boss, presumably reducing the likelihood of any one member being issued contradictory commands, and achieving what is called unity of command (Fayol, 1916/1949). Alternatively, a matrix structure may reinforce strong hierarchical patterns by formally organizing employees into two overlapping networks with two bosses (a functional network including similar and related occupational specialties and a production network linking everyone who works on a product line).

*Span of control* refers to the designated number of subordinates reporting to any given supervisor. Span of control is a critical building block of organizational networks because it has the effect of determining the general shape of the organization. Where span of control is narrow, there tends to be a large number of hierarchical levels, thus producing a "tall" organization with a highly stratified membership such as the armed services, which run from the president of the United States down to the raw recruit. On the contrary, where span of control is wide, there are fewer organizational levels and the overall appearance of the organizational hierarchy tends to be "flat."

The traditional "chain" metaphor is evocative of several important aspects of viewing organizations as networks. First, each dyadic "link" of the chain is affected by every set of interlocking links. Thus we cannot understand any relationship apart from its place within a network. The *"Pelz effect"* (Jablin, 1979; Pelz, 1952), for example, suggests that supervisors who have a great deal of upward influence with those above themselves in the hierarchy tend to have more positive, more motivated, and often more pro-

*Communicative patterns observed at one level of the hierarchy shape configurations at other levels.*

ductive and satisfying relationships with their own subordinates than those supervisors who are perceived to have little influence with those higher up. In other words, the patterns observed at one level shape configurations at other levels.

Second, individuals are continually being pulled in different directions. When we view organizations as elaborated and overlapping personal networks, however, being in the middle is not nearly as problematic as one might imagine. Being in the middle often means having access to dominant coalitions and/or being on a critical path in the work flow. In these cases, the person is more likely to have influence in the organization even if his or her hierarchical level is technically lower than someone who is not as embedded in the system. In a study of a large newspaper publishing company, for example, Brass (1984) found that employees' promotions were strongly associated with the degree to which an individual had a high degree of "network betweenness."

Third, systematic distortion of messages is likely to occur. Messages may be distorted due to the mere number of people the message must pass through (serial transmission) or the inability of a sender or receiver to reproduce the identical message because of cognitive, physical, or social limitations. Specialization, technical vocabulary, and the homogeneous clusters associated with hierarchy increase the likelihood that members of different hierarchical levels are unable to understand how another group thinks or what their messages "mean." From this perspective, leadership becomes "the management of meaning," comprising attempts to guide others across hierarchical boundaries into common definitions and interpretations of reality. Effective leadership, then, depends upon the "extent to which the leader's defi-

nition of a situation . . . serves as the basis of action for others"
(Smircirch & Morgan, 1982, p. 262).

The problems associated with *semantic information distance* are
not necessarily intentionally created but reflect often uncon-
scious and unexpressed conflict of perspectives developed in
most hierarchical networks. For example, Robert Howard (1986)
in *Brave New Workplace* describes how even under the most be-
nign conditions (when system designers are well intentioned and
the workers are most cooperative) there is great difficulty when

---

### MAKING CONNECTIONS

The importance of considering dyadic relationships within larger network patterns can best be illustrated by considering possible conflict
management practices. In Chapter 4, relational complementarity was presented as a significant determinant of the types of conflict strategy interactants chose. Choice of conflict style was shown to be rationally influenced by the symmetrical nature of the dyad.

However, the association between communicative choice and hierarchical position cannot be fully understood by examining dyads in isolation.
Choice is never bound or determined solely by the hierarchical relationship
between two people. It is in the larger context of interconnected relationships that expectations are derived and enacted. In other words, the ways
in which conflict is managed varies with the informal norms that govern
interpersonal networks within and between hierarchical levels.

Morrill (1991), for example, empirically demonstrated that executives
who were embedded in low-density, fragmented, and low-multiplex networks were more likely to handle conflict non-confrontationally than
executives enmeshed in strongly and densely connected networks. He
found that in networks characterized by low degrees of interconnectedness, independence of task, and uniplex relations, managers were more
likely to enact their "social distance and autonomy" by easily withdrawing
from direct confrontation. He suggests that the scarcity of social ties also
decreases the opportunity to mobilize coalitions, minimizing the escalation
and spread of conflict (Gulliver, 1979). Further, loosely knit networks are
less likely to develop an agreed-upon vision of "what is worth fighting for"
and hence avoidance or tolerance of conflictual views is more easily
accomplished.

Networks that are dense, exhibit high degrees of multiplex communication, and are interdependent tend to enact more confrontational forms
of conflict. Within these network structures, it is more likely for a culture
to have a highly developed sense of "what is right" and "what is intoler-
able." Acceptable solutions may take on a win-lose or compromise character but either way the conflict is more likely to be publicly addressed
(Baumgartner, 1988).

computer systems designers try to automate a job process based upon workers' own reports of how they do a job. Howard's analysis assumes (and network analyses suggest he is right) that technical and non-technical employees rarely ever talk to one another in any context. They develop radial, non-overlapping networks that strongly influence interpretive processes. Howard writes:

> There is a gap in world views between those who design the new technology and those who use it. The designer and the office worker are like foreigners speaking different languages, with the added complication that each of them uses the same words to mean entirely different things. (1986, p. 67)

Such unintentional and unidentified semantic gaps result in what some system designers call "automating a fiction." That is, when workers are unable to provide the system designer with messages that can delineate to the outsider what they actually do, they give descriptions that reinforce the analyst's interpretation of how workers perform their jobs. Thus the automated versions

---

### MAKING CONNECTIONS

Rhetorical theorist *Kenneth Burke* (1969) argues that *"mystery"* is a "corresponding condition" to hierarchy. He describes how in hierarchical organizations, that is, organizations with extended chains of command, those at the top become mysterious to those further down and those at the bottom remain enigmatic to those above them. "Mysteries will arise socially," says Burke, "from different modes of life. The king will be a mystery to the peasant and vice versa" (p. 116).

Communication scholars Tompkins, Fisher, Infante, and Tompkins (1975) explored the reciprocal mystery between those at the bottom and those at the top of the hierarchy in a university setting. They found that individuals' perceptions of the degree of mystery in the upper levels varied according to the individuals' rank in the system. Students, non-teaching professionals, and faculty felt the university hierarchy was more secretive and less visible than did other university officials.

Like strategic ambiguity (discussed in the earlier chapter on messages), mystery can have both positive and negative effects. Burke explains that by maintaining cultural cohesion and unity of action mystery serves to induce cooperative action. However, it also inhibits criticism of those at the top by those at the bottom.

of jobs are "out of sync" with the way the jobs actually get accomplished.

Hierarchical networks also maximize the likelihood that messages will be intentionally distorted. The highly segmented networks associated with mechanistic systems are more prone to distortion than the integrated, highly connected networks of organic organizations (Weick, 1987). Relational power, mistrust, high aspiration needs, and insecurity increase the likelihood of distortion. Hierarchical systems also tend to have finely developed norms of secrecy. Status protection norms not only try to ensure face-saving for those higher up but also put each person in his or her place in the sense that certain "highly sensitive" information is only exchanged with people at certain levels of the hierarchy (Sitkin, 1989).

Overall, hierarchical networks serves two basic interdependent functions—*control* and *prediction*. Hierarchical communication enables the dominance of a particular interpretive frame, the

---

### MAKING CONNECTIONS

Highly stratified personnel systems create finely tuned control systems based upon their ability to isolate workers, create semantic information distance, and preempt the kind of coalition building necessary for resistance to authority and change. Edwards (1981) describes such a control system that operated at Polaroid Company.

"With eighteen different job families, three hundred job titles, and fourteen different pay grades, not to mention the dichotomy between salaried and hourly workers, it might appear that Polaroid had gone far enough in dividing and redividing its workers. Not so: each job is now further positioned along the pay scale so that for any given job, seven distinct pay steps are possible, from entry level through 5 percent increments to the top pay for the job. Thus are established more distinct slots. . . . Taking just the job titles and pay steps and ignoring job families classification, Polaroid has created roughly 2,100 individual slots for its 6,397 hourly workers. And that leaves out a number of ancillary means of further dividing workers—the seniority bonus, 'special pay' status, the incentive bonus and so on" (p. 134).

By separating workers both vertically and laterally, Edwards suggests Polaroid could effectively break up the homogeneity of the workforce and raise barriers to alternative forms of job identity and loyalty. In other words, they deliberately create mystery.

inculcation of specific organizational premises or bases for action, the reinforcement of taken-for-granted organizational routines, the creation of identity, and the assignment of meanings to
events. Weick (1987) argues that interpersonal communication is
the essence of organizations because it creates structures that
then affect what else gets said and done and by whom. Structures
form when communication uncovers shared occupational specialties, shared social characteristics, or shared values that people
want to preserve and expand. The structures themselves create
additional resources for communication such as hierarchical levels. These additional resources constrain subsequent contacts
and define more precisely the legitimate topics for further communication.

Hierarchies make organizational behavior more predictable,
creating routines that produce automatic responses to standard
events and socializing members into sets of patterned responses.
Hierarchical divisions and boundaries provide ways for organizations to assign tasks and responsibilities. The more routinized
and rule-bound, the less likelihood of surprises, confusion, and
chaos. The blueprint for rewards, promotion, and advancement
associated with many lockstep hierarchical systems allows individuals to plan and predict their futures.

Paradoxically, the degree to which hierarchical communication
effectively predicts and controls organizational behavior limits
the degree to which organizations can be innovative, flexible, and
responsive, thereby limiting organizational effectiveness in a
rapidly changing environment. Thus, although hierarchy has
served the powerful elite well in the past, highly stratified hierarchical systems are being challenged. Companies are "delayer-
ing" their structure, "re-engineering" their systems, "flattening"
their organizational design. For example, when Dupont's upper
management decided they had developed into a highly bureaucratic, risk-aversive firm that stifled innovation, they changed
their hierarchical structure by reducing managerial levels, going
from eight levels of supervision to four, decentralizing decisions,
and pushing responsibility downward.

But it is not only the precarious link between efficiency and
innovation that is troubling organizations today. The second

strain that is making hierarchical networks less effective and less preferred has to do with the changing workforce described in Chapters 1 and 2. Although adhering to the chain of command and communicating within a predetermined set of links and limited range of content has been traditionally accepted as the way things "should be," many people entering organizations today show less tolerance for organizational structures that isolate them from key decision makers. Workers are demonstrating a greater willingness to act by stepping outside the chain of command and going directly to the top (Hall & Richter, 1990). People no longer accept the implicit, and at times explicit, racism, sexism, and homophobia that have been associated with tradi-

---

### MAKING CONNECTIONS

The increasing number of older workers who remain in the workforce has resulted in several changes in organizational communication that are disconcerting to many people. The traditional hierarchical model that accommodated larger numbers of young entry-level cohorts and smaller numbers of employees at more advanced career stages is outdated. In the conventional model, which mirrors the experience of hierarchy outside the workplace, older workers were expected to supervise younger workers, and seniority was closely associated with organizational rank.

However, the higher educational level of younger employees coupled with their familiarity with new technology and computer literacy has resulted in a reversal of roles, and more and more young people are supervising older workers. This results in great discomfort for many employees. A restaurant manager describes giving orders to older workers as "sort of like telling your grandma to clean the table." A man who returned to the workforce after finding that his pension and other retirement benefits were unable to sustain his lifestyle explains, "When you're being supervised by someone younger you see a lot of things aren't going to work but you have to bite your tongue" (Hirsch, 1990, cited in Jackson, 1992, p. 25).

Unions have also had to adjust to the "graying" of the workforce. Concessions have been made on seniority privileges. In some companies, older workers have had to accept lower wages, and many feel that collective bargaining has turned its back on the older worker (Parker & Slaughter, 1988). The implementation of pay for knowledge schemes, the elimination of absentee replacement workers, even the team concept itself, which often demands job rotation, has made it extremely difficult for older workers to maintain their positions in the organizational hierarchy.

tional hierarchical structuring. Furthermore, the "new career-ism" of the 1980s has democratized the workplace insofar as

*Today's employees are challenging the legitimacy and importance of the formal organizational hierarchy.*

people, regardless of occupation or job level, have taken greater control of their own progress and no longer assume that the organization will take care of its employees in a paternalistic manner (Feldman, 1988).

Moreover, although a large majority of employees are still striving for advancement, employees are challenging the legitimacy and singular importance of the formal hierarchy itself. The "myth of separate worlds" is no longer accepted. Many people born after 1960 have not been socialized in the strong hierarchical systems of the past. Some of these workers are no longer willing, or expected, to be unilaterally committed to climbing the organizational ladder. Kiechel (1989), in describing the "baby boomer" generations—

---

### MAKING CONNECTIONS

Organizational responses to the "balanced-life dilemma" faced by employees include the institutionalization of "job sharing," in which two people do one full-time job, and the creation of the "mommy track." Those workers who opt to job share or go on the mommy track are no longer considered part of the dominant coalitions but are enmeshed in parallel networks in which they are not expected to face the same demands as those on the traditional career track. These workers remain outside the traditional hierarchy insofar as they no longer are looking to move up but to remain within the hierarchy insofar as they keep their job and many of their responsibilities.

For some, the mommy track is seen as a positive step forward, one that accommodates women's needs to achieve success in a variety of contexts, a means of being removed from the pressures of the fast track without having to get out of the race completely, a way of acknowledging their desire to be mothers and work outside the home. For others, the mommy track is seen as a dangerously sophisticated attempt to restore discrimination against women. After years of fighting for equal opportunities in the workplace, critics suggest the mommy track systematically denies woman access to the upper echelons of corporate America. By going on the mommy track, women lose their place, they are no longer seen as a dependable link in the chain.

that is, managers hired in the 1970s— reports: "They don't like telling others what to do any more than they like being told. No respecters of hierarchy, they don't want to get to the top just because it is the top" (p. 58). Many people are frustrated by the conflict in trying to build both a successful career and a successful home life. A *New York Times* Labor Day survey ("Poll Finds," 1989) of over 1,500 men and women indicates that almost half of the women and a third of the men believe that women have had to give up too much in their quest for better jobs and more opportunities. The positive relationships between hierarchical level, performance, and satisfaction found in the past are being somewhat altered.

Thus the bounded, centralized, segmented, vertically differentiated hierarchical networks associated with instrumental, uniplex, and complementary relations seem outdated and inappropriate for organizations of the 1990s. The next chapter will address issues of participation and the creation of networks that are richer, multiplex, and symmetrical. But whether the failure to observe, accept, enact, or design a chain of command has the effect of actually softening the hierarchical structure of organizations or is detrimental to individuals who opt to do so remains to be seen. Edwards (1979) suggests that the degree to which employees endeavor to achieve organizational democracy is closely associated with the degree to which they experience job security. At the very time when companies are publicly trying to do away with at least some hierarchical practices, more and more jobs are in jeopardy, and the gaps among hierarchical levels (in areas such as health care benefits, insurance, family leave, housing, educational opportunities) are greater than ever.

## ❑ Final Connections

Both sustained by and sustaining the central elements of organizations—relationships and messages—hierarchy is an important thread woven into the organizational tapestry. In this chapter, we have examined the structural and emergent features of hierarchies, exploring the ways in which our social affiliations create, re-create, and alter networks of graded relationships. *Hierarchies are powerful organizational structures that are constituted and reconstituted through interpersonal communication.*

Our understanding of hierarchy, however, is clearly complicated and limited by the tensions arising from the constraining and enabling forces embedded within these intersecting networks. *Hierarchies offend our democratic sensibilities but our actions reinforce their presence.* At the very least, the realization of what we do and why we do it enables us to live with the tensions hierarchical systems create. At best, such insights create frameworks for both individual and collective transformation within the rich texture of organizational life. *Hierarchies are resistant to change but are continually changing.*

# Participation

*This chapter focuses upon patterns of interaction that provide alternatives to hierarchical organizations. The complex, interconnected, heterogeneous linkages that constitute participation networks enrich and potentially empower individuals, organizations, and society.*

This chapter is about *participation,* a term rich with potential meanings and a process fundamental to individual, group, and organizational experience. From our earliest connections in our family to our involvement in schools, clubs, and organizations, participation provides an opportunity to discover ourselves in working with others. Participation in small groups elicits a sense of identity and community and facilitates coordination and integration. Many organizational scholars predict that by the twenty-first century successful companies will have "reengineered" their corporations and converted to work teams or other participatory group structures, completely eliminating hierarchical systems

(Hammer & Champy, 1993). A focus on "total quality management" means a focus on teamwork and group interactions.

Americans are ambivalent about participation in groups. De Tocqueville (1840/1945) noted in the early eighteenth century that the United States was a nation of joiners, continually organizing new associations and participating in old ones. Yet, unlike many cultures where the family, tribe, or other form of social collectivity takes precedence over the individual, American society exalts the role and rights of the individual. To become enmeshed in networks, to act collectively, an individual must often subordinate his or her needs and desires to the "will of the group," a process that is often as difficult and frustrating as it is positive and rewarding. Just as social stigma may be attached to being a non-participant or "loner," people who are perceived as belonging to "too many" groups or entangled in "countless" networks are frequently belittled and referred to as "social butterflies" or "groupies."

*Participation* is an ambiguous term. It may denote, among other things, membership in a group or general involvement in group activities, or it may refer more narrowly to involvement in decision making. For instance, you might be part of an academic honor society but not feel that you actually participate in the group if all you do is go to meetings and listen to the officers tell of the decisions that were made. Alternatively, you may rarely attend the meetings or fund-raising activities of your local Amnesty International chapter but feel an active participant because you join in the decisions about the letter writing campaigns.

Participation in the American workplace typically refers to participation in decision making. Moving beyond the small and routine decisions required by a particular job, participation in decision making addresses involvement in broader issues such as job assignments within a given production process, the right to stop an assembly line if something is jeopardizing the quality of the product, or having a say in the way performance appraisals are carried out. Rarely, however, does participation mean management's sharing power to make strategic and long-range decisions. These decisions are considered to be "management's prerogative."

This limited form of participation, or "employee involvement" as it is often called, became a "hot topic" for American social scientists, managers, consultants, and unions looking for a quick answer to the Japanese challenge in the mid-1970s. Concomitant with the "loss of the competitive edge," there was a growing realization that blue- and white-collar workers often know better than management about what to do and how to do it. Managers came to see that employees contribute more to the "bottom line" when their minds as well as their hands are engaged. As organi-

*Participation networks enhance an organization's capacity to respond quickly and creatively.*

zations continue to diversify, respond to the need to innovate and to react flexibly to the uncertain environment of the 1990s, and focus directly on quality control, more and more attention has been put on the organization's communication system; that is, on the purposive development and reinforcement of richer, more diverse, and loosely connected participation networks.

The emerging "global information society" (by the year 2000 over two thirds of American jobs will be in the information sector) is also providing a powerful impetus to what Cleveland (1985) calls "the twilight of hierarchy" and the dawn of participation. Information is a different type of resource than materials such as rubber or gold. Information is shared rather than exchanged (i.e., when I give it to you, we both have it), diffuse rather than limited (i.e., when it leaks, there is more rather than less of it), and it cannot be owned (i.e., you may own a book but you cannot own the facts, ideas, and content contained within). Thus hierarchy, which is most often based on the attainment and control of limited resources, is no longer useful or appropriate. Cleveland (1985) suggests that

> collegial, not command structures become the more natural base for organisation. Not "command and control" but conferring and "networking" become the mandatory modes for getting things

done. . . . The push for participation . . . and the inherent leakiness of the information resource, combine to produce the modern executive's most puzzling dilemma: How do you get everybody in on the act and still get some action? (pp. 188-189)

In this chapter, we will define participation, explore the ways in which it is communicatively constituted, and explore its importance for ourselves and contemporary organizations. Three prototypical participatory networks will be examined: (a) task, (b) social, and (c) occupational. Participation, we shall see, is an

---

## MAKING CONNECTIONS

Organizations throughout the world are attempting to restructure communication patterns and activities to flatten hierarchies, decentralize decision making, and increase organizational flexibility. General Motors, Rolls Royce, Ford, AT&T, the United Auto Workers, the Communication Workers of America are just a few of the large organizations involved in joint management-union quality of work programs that are designed to enhance employee participation in decision making.

There are several alternatives to "top-down management." Many organizations still retain traditional hierarchical networks but develop opportunities for employees to become involved as an add-on to their regular responsibilities. Other corporations radically change the work processes and build employee involvement into the day-to-day routine activities. In some European countries, the law mandates that companies have some form of steering committee or works council on which employee representatives serve and participate in long-term strategic decision making. Listed below are just a few of the better-known companies that are experimenting with different forms of worker participation.

- Shell Oil, Staley's, Cummins Engines, TRW, General Motors, and Procter & Gamble have built new plants using sociotechnical systems that minimize the distance between workers and managers and maximize worker's participation in the day-to-day decisions that affect their jobs.

- By 1986, over 10 million workers in more than 8,000 American companies were participating in employee ownership plans (ESOPs). For example, in 1987 Avis was bought by its 12,500 employees, technically making the workers the bosses of management.

- Beginning in the 1970s Firestone, Citibank, and Ford were among hundreds of companies to implement quality circles to improve quality of production. Voluntary groups comprised of 10-12 workers from the same work area, quality circles are supplemental to the *everyday* work process. Circles are limited in the types of problems they are allowed to address and constrained by the need to get management's approval to implement suggestions

interactive process shaped by multiple strands of activities. It is a complex communication process that blurs the boundaries between what is public and what is private.

## ❑ What Is Participation?

From a network perspective, participation is *constituted by the discretionary interactions of individuals or groups resulting in cooperative linkages that exceed minimal coordination needs.* Participation entails far more than minimal involvement in decision making and affects more than an organization's productivity. The complex, interconnected, heterogeneous linkages that comprise participation networks enrich and potentially empower individuals and society. People learn how to contribute and understand what it means to participate in a community, in part, by what they learn in the workplace. Pateman (1970) persuasively argues that the lack of opportunity to participate in the traditional hierarchical workplace socializes people into passivity and apathy in the political and social sphere. According to Deetz (1992): "The workplace is a site of learning" (p. 38) that transcends organizational boundaries. He suggests "it is likely that authoritarian work structures create more authoritarian child rearing practices" (p. 39). Because non-participatory jobs lead to psychological and physical dysfunctions, many people believe participation issues are more moral than economic in character (Sashkin, 1984). Participation, for many, is a fundamental social right that has value in and of itself.

*Participatory practices transcend organizational boundaries.*

It is a major anachronism of American society that democracy is defined as relevant only in the political sphere of life. The relative freedom of the political arena stands in sharp contrast to the authoritarian principles governing the American workplace. Clearly, a strong case can be made for bringing greater democracy into the workplace in order to create a citizenry that participates in all of the major areas affecting its daily circumstances and its future. (Gamson & Levin, 1984, p. 232)

Clearly, participation can take on many different meanings, assume many different forms, and serve a variety of purposes. For example, when the harmful and alienating aspects of the industrial revolution first became apparent in the first half of the nineteenth century, social activists in Europe looked to some form of worker participation as a means of reintegrating the urban working class into society (Lindenfeld & Rothschild-Whitt, 1982). In the early days of Taylor's (1911/1947) scientific management, employers wanted workers to participate in establishing the most efficient way to perform a particular task by sharing their knowledge of work practices, that is, their "rules of thumb." The goal was efficiency. The Human Relations tradition emphasized the value and potential of participation, cooperation, and collaboration between and among employees. Extensive, open, friendly, trusting, face-to-face encounters between workers and managers were associated with increasing psychological satisfaction, development and growth of individuals, and increased productivity and efficiency of organizations. Increasing worker participation in semi-autonomous work groups was expected to make organizations more competitive in the global economy. Feminist organizations alter traditional networks of authority and hierarchy through shared and revolving leadership so as to provide the opportunity for all groups to participate. The goal is empowerment.

Obviously, simplistic notions of participation as "meaning" upward communication that gives feedback about job procedures does not fully capture critical aspects of the process of participating. To understand and interact in today's organizations, it is essential to understand the various meanings and components of participation.

Participation was not invented by social scientists or management theorists. Workers have always been participating in organizations. Even in the most bureaucratic and mechanized systems, people go beyond their prescribed roles and tasks, developing relationships that cross domains, making decisions and performing actions that have not been completely bounded, anticipated, or programmed. When "participation" doesn't occur, and employees do only what their job descriptions and hierarchical position specify, organizations basically cease to function. In countries where public employees are denied the right to strike, job actions called "work to rule" may be used to paralyze the system. That is, when policemen, railway workers, public transit workers, and other civil employees only work and

---

## MAKING CONNECTIONS

*Rensis Likert,* a professor at the Institute for Social Research at the University of Michigan, is best known for his organizational research program and survey feedback methodology begun in the 1950s. In his classic text *New Patterns of Management* (1961), Likert examines four systems of management, as follows:

System 1: Exploitative-authoritative

System 2: Benevolent-authoritative

System 3: Consultative

System 4: Participative

Each of these systems is based upon the type of communication that goes on between workers and management. Likert was especially concerned with issues related to organizational climate including the degree to which superiors listen to subordinates, the degree to which organizational members are kept informed about specific topics, and the degree to which management is receptive to suggestions, opinions, and ideas

Likert was a strong proponent of participative systems, believing such systems were most effective. He developed a Profile of Organizational Systems, a survey that "diagnoses" whether or not participative values permeate six areas of organizational experience: leadership, motivation, communication, decisions, goals, and control. Likert's ideas about System 4 management and organizational communication were extremely influential. We can find, for example, great parallelism between his notions of participative systems and Redding's (1972) dimensions of the "ideal communication climate": (a) supportiveness, (b) participative decision making, (c) trust, confidence, and credibility, (d) openness and candor, and (e) high performance goals.

communicate according to what the rules say they should do, the entire system begins to shut down. Imagine the impact you and your fellow students, friends, or family members would have on the university, your sorority or fraternity, and your household if you limited your communication and activities to what was explicitly defined by your role.

---

## MAKING CONNECTIONS

*Eric Trist* and his colleagues at the British Tavistock Institute were among the first researchers to highlight the interdependence between the social system and the technical system. In the 1950s they studied the effect of mechanization on miners in the British coal mines. Prior to mechanization, work was controlled by the work group responsible for mining a particular coal seam. Through informal communication and adaptation, the members of each work group would assign and coordinate the necessary tasks among themselves, following the mining of a seam through from beginning to end. Mechanization shattered the cooperative dynamics of the informal work group. Division of labor was formalized, and individual miners were isolated, separated by task, by location on the coal seam, and by shift. Miners no longer had the opportunity to see their efforts carried through to completion. The increased productivity expected to result from mechanization did not occur.

These scholars discovered that no formally designated coordination mechanism could replace the participation and mutual adjustment of the miners. Direct supervision was ineffective because of the dark, dangerous conditions of the mine and the distance between miners. Output measures were ineffective because problems could not be traced to a particular worker or work process. Workers had no sense of being a part of the whole. Mechanization had eliminated an informal communication system without providing a formal replacement, resulting in both lowered productivity and increased worker alienation.

Trist (1963) proposed a solution to bring the formal technical system into accord with the informal communication system of the miners. Work duties were organized to allow small work groups to employ the new technology. Work groups could share jobs, communicate informally, and solve problems as they arose. At the same time, the performance of the group could be measured and standardized. They coined the term *sociotechnical system* to describe this network of semi-autonomous participatory work groups. The term now designates a general concern with the interrelations of the technical and social psychological organization of industrial production systems.

## MULTIPLE PARTICIPATION
## NETWORKS EXIST

Just as there are multiple hierarchies operating in an organization, there are multiple participation networks. Three prototypical participation networks—*task, social,* and *occupational*—that comprise overlapping, collaborative relations are discussed below. Clearly, not everyone has equal access to these networks. Involvement in one facilitates involvement in another. Activities in one network may preclude activities in another. Hierarchical patterns, positional roles, gender and racial segregation, as well as informational gaps and differential experiences are difficult to change. Individuals are constrained by other alignments. Time use studies, for example, find that working men have between 16 and 30 hours per week more time to devote to leisure than working women (Hochschild, 1989). Young, ambitious junior executives may be both willing and able to invest enormous amounts of times and energy in various participation networks, but as these workers age, they may face the dilemmas of those "married with children." Many individuals in midcareer who are "sandwiched" between the demands of children and the needs of aging parents do not have the time or energy to develop any but the most essential organizational linkages. Resistance to participation by one's spouse and family can create strong ambivalence about participation for the organizational member.

It is important to realize that not everyone *wants* to become enmeshed in issues and relationships that go beyond their own particular assignment. Too much participation can contribute to burnout, substance abuse, stress-related physical problems, and family and marital tensions. Rosen, Klein, and Young (1986) point out that even when people own part of the company, participation may be of only minimal interest. "Like members of most democratic organizations, it seems [Employee Stock Ownership Plan] members very rationally hope that their organizations will run well without their having to get too involved, although they may want the power in reserve to change things if needed" (p. 53).

*Task participation networks.* Task participation networks comprise linkages and communicative practices that are rooted in work processes but go beyond those minimally necessary for carrying out one's actual job. These linkages can arise from informal and unstructured interactions or formally designed participatory

---

## MAKING CONNECTIONS

The tension created by demands for participation at home and at work has been the subject of numerous plays, novels, and movies. The classic play *Death of a Salesman* (1952) shows the empty desperation of a man who has given all and lost much in his attempt to participate fully in his work for the company. The 1960s blockbuster movie *The Graduate* humorously portrays the serious alienation and personal sacrifices embodied in the demands of "making it" in the corporate world. In the 1970s *Kramer vs. Kramer* focused on a divorced father's problems as he tried to juggle responsibilities at work and at home. His loss of prestige, clients, income, and self-respect are closely associated with his inability to participate fully in each domain of his life. And the film *Parenthood* (1989) shows how one father has to give up opportunities for advancement at work as he chooses to spend more time with his troubled family and less time dazzling his boss with 70-hour weeks.

In the best-seller *Soul of a New Machine* (1981), Tracy Kidder recounts the efforts of Data General to create a new generation of computers and vividly captures the boundary pressures encountered in a highly participative organization.

"Going to work for the Eclipse Group could be a tough way to start out your profession . . . [Y]ou are told that you have almost no time at all in which to master a virtual encyclopedia of technical detail and to start producing crucial pieces of a crucial new machine. And you want to make a good impression. So you don't have time to meet women, help your wife buy furniture for your apartment, or to explore the unfamiliar countryside. You work" (p. 60).

But perhaps nowhere is the merging of task and social participation as overwhelming as it is in Japan. In Japan, corporate loyalty is often measured by how many hours one puts into the job and this includes obligatory dinner and drinking sessions. It is not unusual for Japanese "salarymen" (i.e., white-collar workers and middle-level managers) to put in over 110 hours of overtime per month. There are many negative consequences associated with this high degree of worker participation (Tubbs, 1993). Indeed, *Karoshi*, literally meaning death from overwork, is such a serious problem that the Japanese government has begun a study to see if they are, indeed, participating "too much" and working themselves to death. In 1990 more than 1,300 families sought advice on filing claims against companies because of death due to overwork (Hiroshi, 1991).

interventions. These extra-task-based interactions create patterns of communication that refine and extend coordination between and among organizational participants. Extraorganizational linkages are often part of these networks, expanding the knowledge base and bringing new ideas, perspectives, and expertise to the organization. For example, a quality circle group may be able to finish a management presentation only when a member's husband (who does not work for the company) is willing to take their work home and draw the detailed diagrams they need to illustrate their proposal. A representative of the chamber of commerce may need to have his spouse participate in a dinner party celebrating and cementing the decision to bring a Japanese automobile plant to his midwestern community so that the Japanese executive's wife would feel welcomed and accepted in the community.

Very often the intensity of participation changes uniplex relationships into multiplex linkages. Providing input at a formal meeting with organizational leaders or working in a problem-solving group gives an individual a chance to demonstrate his or her abilities and interests and forge new personal and professional relationships. Workers may never before have had the chance to talk with managers about issues beyond their own limited jobs. Opportunities to participate often mean opportunities to get to know others across the organization. The greater degree to which participation enriches and extends employee networks and increases both strong and weak ties, the more likely the individual and/or work group will obtain the knowledge, diversity of perspectives, resources, and support necessary to solve problems effectively.

Participatory networks can and do serve to enhance the performance of both individual members and the organization as a whole. Participation provides the opportunity for employees to voice their concerns and explicate their needs. In many organizations, employee assistance programs, flexible work arrangements, and other quality of life initiatives would not have come about if employees did not participate in task forces and other organizational activities that went beyond their own job requirements. These activities are time consuming and demand commitment on the part of all those involved. Immediate rewards are often difficult to see, but over the long term semantic distances are bridged, narrow perspectives are broadened, experiences are enriched, and the organization becomes more responsive to collective needs.

---

### MAKING CONNECTIONS

Despite the many worker benefits promised by advocates of participation, some employees fear its potential consequences. Consider the discussion between Maggie, a garment worker in her sixties, and a teacher in a union labor education class described in the recent book *Participating in Management: Union Organizing on a New Terrain* (Banks & Metzgar, 1989, p. 33).

"Maggie had told the class about her ability to sew the crotch in men's pants better and faster than any other worker because of her trick in making a 'bubble.' For years the company had tried to have the industrial engineers find out Maggie's trick so they could teach all the other workers and raise the production quotas for the entire division. Maggie never let the industrial managers see how she did the bubble; she said knowing the trick allowed her to pace herself, help others who fell behind, and made her feel good about herself and her job. A few days after this confession, the teacher was describing participative management.

"Maggie: I don't see how this participative management stuff is so different from scientific management. They couldn't get my trick by watching me, so now they're going to get me in one of those small groups and get me to *tell* them. No way, I'm not that dumb. Nobody's that dumb.

"Teacher: You might not give up your trick because you know how valuable it is. But . . . the group could put a lot of pressure on you to give up your trick. What if the company were threatening to close the plant?

"Maggie: I've never told anybody and I've had lots of pressure from my workmates to tell. . . . My idea is that when I retire I'll show one person how to do it—it's simple to do. . . . But it's got to be somebody responsible —somebody who will know how to use it.

"Teacher: But what if the plant were going to be shut down? Let's say the company said that unless it was able to reduce costs by $1 million, it was going to shut down the plant. Let's say the union had their own experts examine the company's books and the union concluded that the threat was real. And let's say the company said your trick was worth a million dollars to that plant. Would you give it to them then?

"Maggie: NO!

"Teacher: Huh?

"Maggie: I would never give it to them. Once they have it, it's theirs. They can do anything they want with it. They can use it at another plant and shut ours anyway. What I'd do is I'd get a group of the best workers together, in the union hall, and I'd tell them, and I'd make them swear they would never tell management. The company could have their million dollars, if that would save the plant, but I'd never give them my trick."

But increased participation is not the panacea for all organizational problems. When there are conflicting and adversarial interests within the organization, participatory linkages often threaten workers' autonomy. Workers recognize that, once they share their knowledge with management, the employees are no longer needed and can be replaced by less knowledgeable, less costly workers. Networks therefore may develop to resist the controlling efforts of others (Jermier, 1988).

---

### MAKING CONNECTIONS

*Empowerment* and *personal control* are terms often associated with the new participatory emphasis in the organizations of the 1990s. Both management and employees talk about shared decision making as a way to bring workers' voices into the system and create organizations that are open, sensitive, and responsive to workers' needs and ideas. But is this really what happens?

Several scholars suggest that the communicative practices associated with many high-involvement innovations merely change the way control is enacted rather than actually freeing workers from the "iron cage of bureaucracy" (Barker, 1994). Rather than being a form of human relations, these participative interventions are actually examples of "inhuman relations" (Grenier, 1988).

In contrast to the obvious control mechanisms of traditional bureaucracies, participation may unobtrusively control employees' behavior by controlling their decisions, that is, through *concertive control* (Tompkins & Cheney, 1985) For example, the degree to which employees participate in networks that collaboratively develop norms and rules that have internalized organizational values, the more likely they will make decisions that conform to these values (Cheney, 1983). Strong identification with team members, peer pressure, personal investment in the rules that have been developed, and consensual decision making all combine to make this form of control very powerful. Barker (1994) contrasts this type of control—*concertive control*—with three traditional strategies of control described by Edwards (1981).

| Simple Control (Edwards, 1981) | Technological Control (Edwards, 1981) | Bureaucratic Control (Edwards, 1981) | Concertive Control (Barker, 1994) |
|---|---|---|---|
| direct | machine demands | hierarchical | consensual rules |
| authoritarian | work processes | relations | normative |
| personal | layouts | rational | ideology |
| face-to-face | assembly lines | procedures | collaborative |
| | | impersonal | indirect |
| | | rules | (group pressure) |
| | | sanctions | peer initiated |

Managers and management theorists have long recognized the power and potential challenge of participation networks. Some have tried to preempt their formation by placing restrictions on communication, such as banning conversation among workers on the production line or making discussion of certain topics (production rates, salary levels, work process shortcuts) a dismissible offense. But the threat of anarchy that many managers associate with less bureaucratic structures is greatly exaggerated. Indeed, there are several studies that indicate the team approach results in tighter controls on workers' action, not less. After an intensive study of a manufacturing company, Barker (1994), for example, concluded that the high levels of employee identification, the high degree of consensus about values, and the personal connections that develop from working on a team create a powerful system of "concertive control" in which workers control and monitor themselves to an even greater extent than found in a typical bureaucratic organization.

*Social participation networks.* Social participation networks emerge from communication practices that are distinct from task-related duties. While organizational membership provides the initial grounds for their development, the assigned tasks of the network members are often secondary to the relationships. The term *camaraderie* might best characterize these relationships. When a member joins a company-sponsored sports team, has drinks after work at the company tavern, or helps a co-worker campaign for a community office, he or she develops multiplex relationships that are often perceived as more intense, supportive, and symmetrical. Participation in these networks often brings employees into contact with one another's families and friends and hence strengthens the relationships between work and home life.

In many ways, the linkages constituting social participation networks are precisely the relationships Weber wished to eliminate from his idealized rational-legal bureaucracy, because they open the organization to problems such as favoritism, nepotism, and prejudice. Quite often organizations are reluctant to promote individuals to supervisory positions within the same unit for fear these previously existing social linkages will impede effective control and fair supervision. Similarly, some organizations discourage "fraternization" across hierarchical lines. Participation in social networks is seen as antithetical to the organization's ability to control individual behavior.

However, as suggested above, social linkages, whether developed from task or other types of activities, potentially further an organization's ability to control unobtrusively individuals. Participation in task and social networks bridges the perceived distances between various groups, blurring "we/they" distinctions, and increases organizational identification and acceptance of organizational premises and values (Tompkins & Cheney, 1985). The camaraderie that emerges spontaneously in work teams along with the responsibility workers have for each other's performance provides social pressure to conform to the rules and regulations that the group itself has created. The controlling nature of friendship networks within organizational settings is further elaborated by Fine (1986): "Friendship relationships help control people in organizations by providing personal motivation to accept the world as it is, rather than disassociate oneself through alienation. Likewise friendship paves the way for the smooth organization of promotions and changes within an organization" (p. 201).

Social participation also tends to open up communicative practices; that is, individuals have greater communicative access to one another and the range of topics is dramatically larger and more personal. For individuals in high-stress positions such as crisis care nursing, police work, and teaching, these networks may provide crucial personal support that allows the individual to continue in the organization. In some organizations, such as volunteer, fraternal, and service organizations, social participation is often the critical factor in retaining membership (Knoke & Wood, 1981). The camaraderie and trust as well as low social distance that are generated in these multiplex relationships also foster what Albrecht and Hall (1991) call "innovative talk." The relations "tend to evolve into cloistered, yet powerful cliques that dominate discussion of new ideas" (p. 275).

Social participation networks may also serve to link and coordinate activities of various organizations. A great deal of empirical data support the idea that extraorganizational social links benefit organizations in several ways. For example, starting with over 1,650 organizational leaders from a midsized midwestern community, Perrucci and Pilisuk (1970) found that 26 people held positions on the boards of at least four voluntary community organizations, such as the United Way, Chamber of Commerce, and YWCA. These 26 interorganizational leaders (IOLs) were compared with 26 leaders who did not have interorganizational linkages (OLs). The IOLs were perceived to be more involved with critical community issues and more powerful than the OLs. Further, the IOLs saw each other socially and were more similar in their views than were the OLs. By virtue of their participation in overlapping networks outside the direct work context, these individuals were also able to bring to their organizations more information about the environment and greater prominence for their companies. More recently, Galaskiewicz and Wasserman (1989) found that business firms were more likely to give charitable contributions to a non-profit organization that was founded by companies whose chief executive officer (CEO) and/or beneficiary officers were known personally.

*Occupational participation networks.* Occupational participation networks comprise linkages and communication practices that are rooted in one's work but that transcend organizational boundaries to reflect and reinforce shared training, shared values, and/or shared worldviews. Involvement in professional organizations (e.g., Certified Professional Secretaries Association, American Bar Association, American Institute of Chemists), unions, and continuing education for certification or licensing regulations are forms of participation that may mediate an individual's perceptions and interpretations of organizational life.

*Occupational networks influence the meaning of work.*

For some professionals, particularly those with independent practices such as lawyers, doctors, or therapists, occupational networks may simultaneously serve as their task and social participation networks. For other individuals, occupational networks may serve to reinforce or weaken their ties to other networks. It has been theorized that the high proportion of professional engineers in the ranks of whistle-blowers may be

---

**MAKING CONNECTIONS**

Social and occupational participation networks often overlap. For example, an elite group of 100 executive secretaries are part of the Seraphic Society, an exclusive New York society that meets regularly to socialize and provide advice to its members. These elite secretaries often feel isolated; because of their bosses' high status and power, no one in the office gossips with them; because they have unique and grave responsibilities, there is no one to share the responsibility.

As with many exclusive clubs, you cannot apply to participate in the society. Members keep track of the secretaries in the finest and most venerable New York organizations and surreptitiously evaluate the candidates for membership. For example, an article in the *Wall Street Journal* describes how Joyce Gibson, assistant to the executive of the Rockefeller Group, was surprised when she was asked to join this club. Weeks before the invitation, "she had unknowingly met six of its members. A secretary she knew had invited her to join some women in the Rainbow Room, a gathering that seemed unremarkable at the time. 'It was a very pleasant lunch', she says. It was also a covert interview. 'I was looked over.' She clearly met the group's standards of communicative competence, if she had not, she would not have been told of the organization or the interview" (p. 10).

But it is not only the secretary herself who must pass the test. The boss's credentials are also subject to review. The boss must be extremely wealthy but also well respected. Buyout kings, young upstart business moguls, headhunters, or people with the slightest scandal surrounding them are disqualified. Even then, the group must be satisfied that the boss's participation in other organizations is "acceptable." His or her memberships on boards of directors (e.g., museums, hospitals, zoological societies) are carefully screened. If the boss dies, as was the case recently of Seraphic boss Malcolm Forbes, the secretary is immediately demoted to associate status.

The Seraphic Society makes great demands upon the secretaries' time; they are expected to attend numerous luncheons and dinners. It also provides them with elegant perks, such as trips on the Forbes yacht (when he was alive), complementary dinners in the most exclusive restaurants, free trips on airlines, and lovely tokens of appreciation such as silk scarves and free samples. Seraphic Society members are part of an elite occupational and social network, one that is clearly predicated on who you know, what you talk about, and how you talk about it (Fuchsberg, 1990, pp. 1, 10. Reprinted by permission from the *Wall Street Journal* © 1990, Dow Jones & Company, Inc. All rights reserved worldwide).

attributable in part to their potent socialization into and identification with the engineering profession, which then outweighs more immediate organizational concerns (Perrucci, Anderson, Schendel, & Trachtman, 1980). In contrast, Schiappa (1989) argues that the engineers at Morton Thiokol were unable to sustain their concerns regarding the *Challenger* launch precisely because they were, by profession and identification, engineers and not management. Engineers are supposed to establish "facts"; management makes decisions. The decision to launch or not launch therefore was not considered within their purview: "The engineers' understanding of their 'place' created an unwillingness 'to cross role boundaries.' . . . Identified as 'engineers' and not as 'management,' the parties involved felt further objection to the launch would have been inappropriate" (Schiappa, 1989, p. 51).

Van Maanen and Barley (1984) contend that when we consider task participation networks we accentuate the meaning that work has for others (e.g., she is an employee of GM). An occupational network, on the other hand, concentrates upon the mean-

---

### MAKING CONNECTIONS

Occupational networks oftentimes hamper corporate innovation because they create stumbling blocks to coordination and communication between divisions. SmithKline Beckman, a Philadelphia pharmaceutical company, learned some expensive and painful lessons about the need for interdivisional communication and support networks. A vaccine for treating certain forms of hepatitis was discovered by corporate researchers in the early 1980s. But SmithKline marketers turned down the idea because the company did not normally sell vaccine in the United States.

"The scientists persisted, siphoning off money from various projects to conduct clinical trials. Even after these tests succeeded, the marketers said no, primarily because vaccines present serious risks of product liability lawsuits. The researchers finally persuaded the company's international division (through interpersonal relationships that were not anywhere on the organizational chart) which already marketed vaccines to give the product a try and success was swift. SmithKline will sell about $50 million of the drug overseas and is finally seeking FDA approval—a two year process. 'Too bad they didn't listen to us a couple of years ago,' says Martin Rosenberg, a SmithKline research Vice President, 'they would have a $100 million drug by now' " (K. Labich, *Fortune*, June 6, 1988, p. 53. Copyright © 1988 Time, Inc. All rights reserved).

ing of the work for those who do it (I am a mechanic regardless of where I work). Their notion of occupational communities "rests [on] the idea that the work we do shapes the totality of our lives, and, to a great extent, determines who we think we are" (p. 293).

Just as with task and social networks, participation in occupational networks may be encouraged or discouraged by the organization as a whole. Members of occupational communities (networks) develop linkages and interpretive codes external to the organization and thereby have potentially powerful resources that may either support or oppose organizational values and procedures (Van Maanen & Barley, 1984).

## ❑ The Emergence of Participation Networks

Participation networks may emerge from (a) intentional interventions by one or more people (e.g., a group of workers form a softball team or management begins a quality circle program) or (b) naturally occurring and spontaneous patterning of interpersonal communication activities (e.g., a group of teachers begin informal problem-solving sessions in the break room and are joined by several clerical workers who just happen to be there at the same time). Membership is less explicit in the unplanned emergent network and seldom acknowledged. What appears to be simply a coffee klatch or three workers standing by the watercooler killing time and gossiping may in fact be a group of co-workers participating in informal problem solving. Participatory leadership may also reflect a generalized pattern of communication, not necessarily associated with a set of specialized interactions. Leadership is participatory insofar as it solicits and elicits employee involvement and collaboration in the work processes and facilitates a climate of cooperation (Likert, 1961).

The key elements in these informal participatory networks are flexibility and responsiveness. Rather than reinforcing *one* way to organize, organizational members do whatever needs to be done. Informal participation produces a rich tapestry of multiplex relationships interwoven across several domains. In many ways, formal participatory systems may only be successful to the degree that informal participatory networks represent the typical way of "doing business." Innovation, creativity, and the synergistic potential of a diverse workforce are dependent upon the development of trusting, supportive, diverse, symmetrical interpersonal connections. Ironically, the reliance and confidence demanded of network linkages in highly participative systems often reinforce the pernicious aspects of traditional organizations in the sense that "who you know rather than what you do" is a strong determinant of organizational entry and success. Pacanowsky's honest description of the way in which he got into W. L. Gore & Associates highlights the importance of extraorganizational network linkages in all types of organizing systems.

---

### MAKING CONNECTIONS

*Rosabeth Moss Kanter*, consultant to some of the nation's top companies, describes the integrated, complicated networks that are indicative of highly participative, high-performing organizations in her best-selling book *The Changemasters* (1983). She argues that "to produce innovation, more complexity is essential: more relationships, more sources of information, more angles on the problem, more ways to pull in human and material resources, more freedom to walk around and across the organization."

In her sketch of "Chipco" (pseudonym for a computer manufacturer that has achieved record-breaking success and considerable notoriety for its sales and profit growth, leadership in affirmative action, responsiveness to minority issues, and excellent personnel benefits), she highlights the degree of relational involvement that transcends the usual chain of command, and the development of communication linkages throughout the organization.

"Employees portrayed Chipco with a variety of vivid images: a family, a competing guild, a society on a secluded Pacific island, a group of people with an organizational chart hung around it, a Gypsy society, a university, a theocracy, twenty five different companies and a company with 'ten thousand entrepreneurs.' Organizational charts drawn by Chipco informants often resembled plates of spaghetti more than a conventional set of boxes. Such imagery described many of the striking features of Chipco; its large number of enterprising employees, their interdependence in a complex matrix organization, the emphasis on knowledge and teamwork, continuing vibrant growth and change, and Chipco's sense of its own uniqueness" (p. 36).

So I went to work at W. L. Gore & Associates. I got in because my brother was a trusted associate of seven years' tenure, and in a company like Gore, who knows you and who will vouch for you is of extreme importance. (Family ties were common at Gore. Bill Gore told me that as many as 55% of the associates in the Delaware Maryland area were related to one another.). (1988, p. 358)

Considering the social, political, and economic environment of the 1990s, it is not surprising that with increasing frequency organizations are prescribing formal participation structures to complement, control, or negate the informal participation that is already taking place. Of course, no formal system can fully account for the networks that develop but a commitment to participation gives sanction to communication activities that would be inappropriate and unthinkable in strong hierarchical networks. For example, quality circles, limited as they are, legitimate an hourly employee's right to ask a plant manager for production figures.

Formal participation systems are of two types. Most common are *interventions*, participation programs in which the hierarchical task structure is softened but remains in place. While workers can stymie implementation of these management-sponsored participation plans, they have few means and no "legitimate" authority to institute, design, or reward such programs themselves. Furthermore, although information and resources are more readily available to all, task activities are expanded, and employee input is sought and encouraged, the upper levels maintain control of defining what are appropriate issues for discussion. For example, in sociotechnical systems, employees may decide how best to accomplish a task but they cannot decide that the task should not be accomplished. In one sociotechnical plant, the managers "allowed" the teams to decide how to maintain a skeletal staff on Christmas Day, but there was no option for "associates" to decide to close the plant completely (Wilson, 1990). Examples of *interventions* include *semi-autonomous work groups* in which many of the responsibilities and obligations of management are reassigned to the team level; *gain-sharing plans* in which workers financially benefit from the high performance of the company; *employee involvement groups*, which are designed to deal with issues of production and quality; *task forces* and *ad hoc committees* that are set up to deal with a specific problem and disband once they have solved the problem; and *company-sponsored support groups* intended to help workers with personal/social problems. Participatory networks may be loosely coupled, parallel to the everyday processes of organizing, or represent the day-to-day way of conducting business.

Formal participation interventions vary on a wide range of communicative dimensions including (a) complexity of the issues in which employees may be involved, (b) the degree to which the enriched networks become institutionalized, and (c) the extrinsic or intrinsic rewards associated with participation. Participation may also be direct or representative. Direct participation refers to those patterns in which all employees are directly involved in the decision-making process. Employees get to talk to more people about more things across the organization. Their networks are expanded, they become more central and interconnected. In representative participation, some employees are given (through elections or some other formal procedure) the authority to decide on behalf of the employees but the communicative patterns of most employees remain stable.

Workers who have the ability to communicate directly in a participatory manner—that is, to talk about issues that go beyond actual job needs, or to be involved directly with day-to-day work process decisions—are more likely to reap personal benefits and experience greater satisfaction than those whose interests are "represented" in the formal system by other workers (Miller & Monge, 1986; Strauss & Rosenstein, 1970). Nonetheless, when hierarchical task networks remain fairly stable, representative forms of participation such as those found in Germany (co-determination) and the Netherlands provide workers with greater opportunities to have a say in wide-ranging strategic decisions such as plant closings, layoffs, or mergers.

As different as each participatory intervention may be, however, they have several things in common that contrast sharply with traditional hierarchies. Research has shown that successful interventions change the way managers manage, workers work, and organizations organize by changing the nature of messages and relationships (Bartlett, 1983; Lawler, 1986; Stohl, 1986b). First, organizational members exchange information and ideas as needed, thus blurring boundaries among specializations, functions, and levels. Second, multiplex, supportive relationships develop as people interact more intensely. Third, networks become richer, more complicated, and less structured. Traditional boundaries are insubstantial and in flux. Fourth, employees' contributions to the organizational conversation are expanded.

*Non-hierarchical organizations* represent the second type of participatory system. These organizations are richly textured, dynamic networks comprising active agents with multiple identities who work out and work on difference (Gottfried & Weiss, 1994). Non-hierarchical organizations may be visionary or pragmatic, religious or secular, what they have in common is the belief in a person's right and obligation to participate in social life. Although similar to interventions in some ways, the major difference is the totality with

> *Non-hierarchical organizations provide alternatives to top-down patterns of communication.*

which participatory processes are embedded in organizational communication. The interdependence among social domains is explicitly acknowledged and networks are recognized for their transforming and empowering nature. As conscious alternatives to top-down patterns of communication and decision making, organizing principles and practices are based upon egalitarian, participatory goals. Some writers have called this alternative to hierarchy a "heterarchy" (Marshall, 1990).

> A heterarchy has no one person or principle in command. Rather, temporary pyramids of authority form when appropriate in a system of mutual constraints and influences. The childhood game of paper, stone and scissors provides a simple illustration: paper wraps stone, stone blunts scissors, scissors cut paper. There is no fixed hierarchy, but each is effective, and recognized in its own realm. (Marshall, 1990, p. 281)

As suggested in Chapter 5, it is difficult for many of us even to imagine that true alternatives to hierarchical organizing could possibly exist. There seem to be very few non-hierarchical organizations that have survived long periods of time. Those that have survived are often perceived to be tightly interconnected networks that are (a) specialized interest groups who do not have to face a competitive environment (support groups like Alcoholics Anonymous), (b) typically homogeneous (all members are "environmental radicals"), (c) religiously based (the Quakers have practiced consensus decision making since their inception in the seventeenth century; Boulding, 1988), or (d) transformed, having compromised their principles to a great extent.

There are, however, several examples of long-standing and highly successful organizations whose communicative patterns are consistent with democratic, egalitarian, participatory principles. Worker cooperatives, owned by the workers who manufacture goods that must be sold in a highly competitive marketplace, give each member an equal voice in operating and investment decisions and in the selection of a board of directors to supervise operations. Leadership is shared and worker-members have residual claims to all earning over non-labor costs. Boundaries are flexible and permeable; workers' social and family needs are considered legitimate arenas for discussion and action. The *kibbutz* system in Israel has lasted over two generations; worker cooperatives in the plywood industry of the Pacific Northwest have survived for over 50 years (Greenberg, 1986); and Mondragon, a vast worker cooperative complex in the Basque Region of Spain, has grown from 23 workers in one cooperative in 1956 to 19,500 workers in more than 100 cooperative sites, producing refrigerators, stoves, electronic components, and other manufactured goods in 1991 (Cheney, 1995; Whyte & Whyte, 1991).

International non-governmental organizations, of which there are over 18,000, also provide several successful models of alternative organizing principles. These organizations are less hierarchically organized, less centralized, and more flexible because of rotating leadership. Their sensitivity to diversity through open dialogue, responsiveness, and consensual decision-making processes is exemplified in organizations such as the Non-Aligned

Movement (NAM) and Sarvodaya International. Descriptions of these organizations always include reference to the highly intense, frequent, and at times, chaotic multiplex communication networks that are enacted (Boulding, 1988).

Feminist organizations also provide alternative models for organizations that are based upon participatory principles, shared leadership, and rotation of responsibilities (Gould, 1979). The integration of emotional as well as rational processes, the emphasis on community and nurturance, and the recognition and celebration of overlapping domains are distinguishing features of these organizations. Like other non-hierarchical systems, feminist organizations often have unsettled boundaries and are in a state of constant flux. New roles and relationships are continually emerging as members try to reconcile diversity with consensus. In a study of a women's organization in a university setting, for example, Gottfried and Weiss (1994) detail the compromise and change that are undertaken to strike a balance between some members' desire for collective leadership and others' needs and concerns for top-down leadership. They created the position of convenor, one who exercises less power and independence than in typically hierarchical organization but shoulders more administrative responsibility than typically allocated in a collective organization.

Clearly, non-hierarchical organizations are as diverse as more traditional organizations. What they do have in common, however, are several network features. First, the mission of the organization is well articulated and embedded within networks. The "compatibility" principle of sociotechnical theory suggests that outcomes of organizational design reflect not only ends but also means. A truly participative social system cannot be created by fiat; it must be arrived at through participative means and developing relationships. In non-hierarchical organizations, the compatibility principle is continually enacted. Information is shared, personal needs are recognized and legitimated, and self-conscious conversations about content and form are common. Dissonance is not only tolerated but encouraged, while agreement is a common goal. Second, the organizations are continually evolving, building coalitions, developing linkages across systems with the intention of maintaining open and diverse networks. The organization is peer driven. Hierarchical forms may emerge but they are episodic reactions to a particular exigency that are reformed when the project is completed. Third, networks are multiplex, decentralized, and flexible. Some scholars suggest they are polycephalous, that is, "many headed," with different people assuming leadership for different tasks (Lipnack & Stamps, 1986). Fourth, and perhaps most striking, is the manner in which participants cohere through shared values and interests. This dynamic equilibrium is brought about through multiple levels of embeddedness and permeability. Connections wax and wane as circumstances and values change, thus membership is always in flux.

---

### MAKING CONNECTIONS

Mumby and Putnam (1992) provide an extended description of Redwood Records, which "illustrates the ways in which egalitarianism, supportiveness, and diversity of interests intertwine to form a profitable organizational community" (p. 477). Their description of this feminist organization illustrates the degree to which a non-hierarchical organizations must build networks with like others to survive.

"Founded as a feminist alternative institution Redwood Records developed a work atmosphere of informality, supportiveness, and consensual decision making aimed at social change. As the organization grew and adapted to changes in the music industry, Redwood experienced tension between profit and its political goals. But by coalition building with similar groups in the industry (e.g., anti-war advocates, environmentalists) and building multiple subcultures, Redwood Records preserved its philosophy and found unity through diversity of interests. The building of coalitions occurred when Holly Near, the founder and major recording artist of Redwood Records made albums that connected anti-war and feminist groups. These productions led to other songs that unified diverse audiences as well as tours that included an array of performing artists who shared concerns for international issues but differed in their political goals. Thus, although Redwood Records experienced the tensions between profits and social change, it broadened its focus to serve multiple interests, and it remained economically solvent without losing its sense of community, egalitarianism and supportiveness" (Mumby & Putnam, 1992, p. 477).

---

## ❏ Consequences of Participation

Participation is a social concept, constituted by communication, which has consequences for the individual as well as the

---

### MAKING CONNECTIONS

The chart below highlights some of the potential outcomes of participation that have been found across organizations. These effects are strongly mediated by the communicative, cognitive, and motivational conditions that develop in the enriched and extended networks associated with participation.

| | | |
|---|---|---|
| | sharing information | |
| | more knowledgeable employees | |
| | expression of diverse opinions | BETTER DECISIONS |
| | sense of cohesiveness | |
| P | | |
| | explanation and understanding of | |
| A | job rationales | |
| | teamwork | |
| R | greater commitment to task/goal | INCREASED |
| | reduced resistance to change | PRODUCTIVITY |
| T | group pressure | |
| I | chance to express oneself | |
| | sense of achievement | JOB SATISFACTION |
| C | rewards of involvement | |
| | social support | |
| I | | |
| | access to decision making | |
| P | recognition and formalization | |
| | of workers' rights | DEMOCRATIZATION |
| A | shared responsibility | OF THE WORKPLACE |
| | open information channels | |
| T | symmetrical relationships | |
| I | needs assessment | |
| | access to strategic decision making | REDISTRIBUTION |
| O | direct incentives for productivity | OF RESOURCES |
| | interdependence | |
| N | | |
| | peer management | |
| | shared value consensus | CONCERTIVE |
| | group pressure | CONTROL |
| | strong identification with the system | |

collectivity. Participation decentralizes, interconnects, and establishes new networks, often breaking down hierarchical boundaries. Traditional perspectives focus upon three basic outcomes from participation in the workplace—better decisions, enhanced productivity/quality, and increased job satisfaction. A network perspective lets us see how outcomes related to increased democratization, empowerment, and individual and collective rights must also be recognized.

## ❑ Final Connections

Participation is essential to the functioning of both individuals and organizations, but the level of participation is highly variable. For individuals, the challenge is one of balancing participation across multiple groups and organizations, often with competing demands. For organizations, the challenge is to induce an optimal level of participation from highly variable individuals and groups with multiple interests and often conflicting goals.

In this chapter, we have examined the forms and functions of participation. *Participation enables us to realize more fully our individuality. Participation simultaneously opens and closes possibilities.* Through active participation, we both enrich and enliven the tapestry of organizational life. By choosing to participate, we empower ourselves, making our organizations more consistent with democratic values and ideals.

# Conclusion

*"Seeing" organizations as networks has given us a way to examine the interplay between individuals and dynamic social structures. In this final chapter, we will explore the implications of the network metaphor for thinking about our own connections to time and space—our connectedness in action.*

This book began with a very simple set of arguments. *Communication takes place at the intersection of contexts, actors, relations, and activities that cannot be disassociated from one another.* Organizational communication is *the collective interactive process of generating and interpreting messages.* The study of organizational communication must take into account *the social matrices in which individuals are embedded.*

"Seeing" organizations as networks moves us away from individual-level explanations to a focus on social embeddedness and connectedness. We have addressed the basic elements of networks—messages and relationships—and examined the interwoven processes of hierarchy and participation. Multiple examples have illustrated that individuals, groups, and organizations do not make decisions or behave independently of social constraints, but neither do they strictly adhere to prescribed behavior associated with specific social roles. Rather, purposive action is always embedded in, and influenced by, overlapping systems of relationships.

In this chapter, we will briefly review the implications of a network metaphor for understanding organizational communication. We will then explore the ethical dimensions of this perspective.  As we shall see, to conceive of our world in terms of our connections produces exciting possibilities and great responsibilities.

## ❑ The Pragmatic Implications of a Network Metaphor

Throughout the text, we have articulated a structural dynamic that captures the richness, complexity, and fragmentation of today's organizations. Networks are collective manifestations of individual choices whose boundaries are stable yet permeable. Public and personal spheres of interaction overlap. The network metaphor gives us a useful set of conceptual tools to understand organizational experiences and develop innovative solutions to contemporary problems. For example, pre- and post-employment drug testing, employee assistance programs, diversity training, and corporate espionage are all communication activities that transcend traditional boundaries. Corporations not only have the technology to monitor the concurrent activities of large numbers of employees without the direct involvement of a supervisor but also have software that allows them to monitor all employee files on the employee's personal computer. These issues can only be addressed by taking into account the multiple networks in which employees and organizations are embedded. It is possible that the close-knit multiplex networks of non-hierarchical organizations may be better able to address and cope with issues of confidentiality and employee privacy in the electronic workplace than traditional hierarchically based standards of appropriateness and privacy.

Focusing upon interconnections also helps us resolve what may seem, at first glance, to be organizational paradoxes. For example, it probably will no longer surprise you to learn that, although the United States is known as a society of litigants and lawyers, there is strong evidence to suggest that not only is the use of lawsuits for breach of contract rare but disputes are frequently settled without even reference to the contract or potential or actual legal sanctions. A network view of organizations guides us to look at the embeddedness of social interaction to understand this type of "non-rational" organizational behavior. Macaulay's (1963) study of business relationships, for example, found that even though turning matters over to an attorney may have seemed the "rational" and efficient thing to do, those involved believed the executives' interpersonal relationships, cultivated in country clubs, forged through joint memberships on government committees, and so on, were so important and would deteriorate to such a degree that the "cost" of a lawsuit would be too great indeed.

> Even where the parties have a detailed and carefully planned agreement which indicates what is to happen, if say, the seller fails to deliver on time, often they will never refer to the agreement but will negotiate a solution when the problem arises as if there never had been any original contract. One purchasing agent expressed a common business attitude when he said, "If something comes up you get the other man on the telephone and deal with the problem. You don't read legalistic contract clauses at each other if he wants to do business again. One doesn't run to lawyers if he wants to stay in business because one must behave decently." (Macaulay, 1963, p. 61)

Just as the settlement of disputes is strongly influenced by the embeddedness of business in social relations, issues of organizational trust and the adoption of legalistic remedies to address

## MAKING CONNECTIONS

Even the most traditional approaches to organizational behavior have begun to incorporate the idea that organizations comprise networks with fluid and permeable boundaries. In a recent study of managerial activities (Kraut, Pedigo, McKenna, & Dunnette, 1989), for example, three distinct levels of managers were identified. Each level of the hierarchy was associated with specific communication activities. As you read each description, note the emphasis on boundary spanning activities.

*First-level managers* deal directly and on a regular basis with lower level employees. Managing individual performance was rated as the most important set of activities. To do this effectively, lower level managers must be aware of employees' connections outside the workplace and be somewhat familiar with the stresses and strains embedded in the network. Activities include motivating employees, providing ongoing performance feedback, taking action to resolve performance problems, blending subordinates' goals with company work requirements, and identifying ways of improving communication among employees.

*Middle managers* are driven by the need to link groups together and are less likely to be directly involved with lower level employee networks. The most important tasks for middle managers involve planning and allocating resources among different groups, coordinating interdependent groups, and managing group performance. Middle-level managers are expected to translate general directives into specific plans and communicate their benefits.

*Upper-level managers*, the executives, are expected, like middle managers, to coordinate interdependent groups. Primarily, however, they are involved in monitoring the business environment through developing and maintaining relationships with the outside business community and participating in task forces to identify new business opportunities and gather information about relevant trends.

The one activity that was perceived as critical for all levels of the managerial hierarchy was "representing your staff, being their ambassador in various settings." This spokesperson role points to the importance for managers at all levels to be enmeshed within multiple intraorganizational and interorganizational networks. The tasks associated with ambassadorship include developing relationships with other managers from other groups, communicating the needs of your group to others, helping subordinates interact with other groups, and acting as the group's representative. The authors speculate that "a big transition takes place when one initially is promoted into management. Until then individuals may have spoken only for themselves, thus some adjustment is required before the manager will recognize and take on the role of group ambassador" (Kraut et al., 1989, p. 289).

organizational problems are also rooted in the configurations of interpersonal linkages. Organizations tend to use legal mechanisms as the mode of control when interpersonal trust is lacking and networks are highly segmented. Granovetter (1985) notes: "The widespread preference for transacting with individuals of known reputation implies that few are actually content to rely on either generalized morality or institutional arrangement to guard against trouble" (p. 490).

*Organizational trust is rooted in the configurations of interpersonal linkages.*

Using the case of Pacific Bell's formal procedures on how to deal with HIV/AIDS employees, Sitkin and Roth (1993) explain the limited effectiveness of legalistic remedies in terms of distrust and interconnections. Pacific Bell was a company that had internal problems and was enmeshed in " 'open warfare' with San Francisco's gay community in relation to HIV/AIDS . . . for example, their exclusionary hiring practices had led to the largest ever settlement in a gay discrimination case—$3 million" (Sitkin & Roth, 1993, p. 367). The legal "solution" to this problem did not

---

### MAKING CONNECTIONS

The awareness of the importance of good relationships that transcend organizational boundaries has driven organizations to forge new connections in areas in which they have never before been involved. For example, companies have now become activists in the political realm, supporting and fighting for specific legislation that may not directly address the companies' needs but will help their customers. These actions are rooted in the conception of customers as links in homogeneous and closely knit networks. By linking themselves with an issue that is supported by potential customers, companies hope the customers will connect with their products.

An exemplar of this indirect corporate communication to a tightly interconnected, select, but unknown network is KING SIZE company. KING SIZE company is a mail order clothing business with an estimated 400,000 customers, which caters to the clothing needs of very tall and large men. In 1991 they began lobbying Congress and airline companies for bigger seats on airlines, more leg room, and other amenities that would appeal to bigger and taller passengers. The management hopes that this political action will build goodwill and provide name recognition for their company with their potential customers (Springen, 1991, p. 51. *Newsweek*, Dec. 16, 1991, Newsweek, Inc. All rights reserved. Reprinted by permission).

address the interpersonal dynamics of workers' internal and external networks at Pacific Bell and hence was ineffective. Sitkin and Roth report that only when management and the union cooperated closely in developing education programs to address directly employee fears and relational concerns within their networks was progress made. Further, and perhaps most important, the company built a coalition with others in the community. They funded and promoted an educational video about HIV/AIDS in the workplace. By directly engaging personal and interorganizational networks, Pacific Bell was able to remedy the distrust of its employees and its publics.

The implications of the network metaphor for understanding organizational communication go even further than connections with the local community. Our values are derived in large part from the national culture in which we are embedded. A survey of over 15,000 executives found that culture of origin was the most important determinant of values (Hampden-Turner & Trompenaars, 1993). Values influence selection of modes, means, and ends of production, preferences and premises about what organizations should and could be, and expectations for the ways in which individuals perform their roles and relate to one another (Hofstede, 1984). To understand organizational communication, we must be especially sensitive to the cultural milieu in which the organization is situated.

Clearly, a network approach to understanding organizational communication helps us recognize that solutions as well as problems can be found in the dynamic matrices of personal networks. Karl Weick (1984) wrote of "small wins," suggesting that the activities we participate in as we go about solving everyday problems may more radically change an organization than grandiose and revolutionary projects. The activities Weick refers to begin and end with changing patterns of communication. Embedded within our networks are essential processes of potential change, emergence, inclusion, and transition.

*Innovative solutions to contemporary problems may be found in the dynamic matrices of personal networks.*

## MAKING CONNECTIONS

Many people would agree that participation in the American workplace is, for the most part, overwhelming. Hard work, commitment, and technology were supposed to bring the rewards of the good life, the opportunity to enjoy our families, the time to be good citizens, and so on. By the time many of us arrive home, however, we are too exhausted to take part in any of these or other activities. Time-saving devices are used so that we can spend more time at work just trying to earn enough money to keep an acceptable standard of living. Direct overtime as well as extra hours spent taking courses for career development and other participatory activities result in many people working 50- or 60-hour weeks.

Several solutions to this problem have been suggested. They range from demands for the return of single-income households to innovative development of time-saving technology to shortening the work-week. This latter suggestion, often met with great skepticism, is certainly the most provocative and perhaps the most far reaching insofar as it has the potential to address several boundary issues.

According to Barbara Brandt, an expert on quality of work life issues, fear for the competitiveness of American corporations in the global community has led many companies to demand longer hours and dismiss the possibility of shortening the work-week, although such a reduction would be consistent with other nations whose productivity is on par with the United States. German workers, for example, average 40 days off a year (twice the American average). A shorter work-week would also possibly result in employment being dispersed more evenly, stemming layoffs and bridging the gaps between those who can find work and those who can't. A shorter work-week could also potentially forge new connections among workers as they learn new ways to coordinate task activities, participating as team members searching for ways to complete tasks effectively and efficiently.

A shorter work-week directly confronts the "myth of separate worlds" that has permeated most organizational decisions. Notice how Brandt's argument is rooted in the recognition that communication and action within one social network have strong implications for what goes on in another.

"The best solution to overwork is a new national policy of fewer work hours for all, with no corresponding loss in pay. Rather than focus on the supposed benefits of the work ethic and ignore the harm caused by overwork, society should support working people's efforts to have more time to nurture their families, keep ties with friends, and give to their communities" (Brandt, 1990, p. 17. This material appeared in *Dollars & Sense*, a popular economics magazine. Subscriptions $18.95 from *D&S*, 1 Summer Street, Somerville, MA 02143).

❑ **A Network Metaphor Enriches
Our Sense of Time and History**

The network metaphor involves us in the past as well as the future. Connectedness in action indicates that organizations are structures with history and continuity. The "quick fix" approach of American management ignores the essential nature of organizational communication. Indeed, a paradox of time exists in the global marketplace of today. Billions of dollars can be transferred in seconds from Paris to San Francisco, people can travel from one continent to another in a matter of a few hours, communication across thousand of miles is instantaneous, and goods can move around the world in a single day. Yet it is American management's short-term thinking, which at first blush seems suited for the fast pace of change, that has been blamed for many of America's organizational ills. Scholars and practitioners alike suggest that this rapidly changing and complex environment must be understood in an expanded time frame.

> *A rapidly changing and complex environment must be understood in an expanded time frame.*

But what is an appropriate time frame in which to situate our views and overall comprehension of organizations? Elise Boulding develops the notion of the "200 year present," a fascinating yet simple idea that is almost revolutionary in its implications for what we do and how we understand organizations and communication.

> That present begins 100 years ago today, on the day of birth of those among us who are centenarians. Its other boundary is the 100th birthday of those babies born today. This present is a continuously moving moment, always reaching out 100 years in either direction from the day we are in. We are linked with both boundaries of this moment by the people among us whose life began or will end at one of those boundaries, five generations each way in time. It is our space, one that we can move around in directly in our own lives and indirectly by touching the lives of the young and old around us. (1988, p. 4)

Think about the world about 100 years ago. All of the countries in the Middle East and South Asia were part of the European empires, the Russian Empire had not been transformed into the Soviet Union, the nations that were to become Yugoslavia after World War I were part of the Ottoman and Austro-Hungarian empires. The International Congress of Women met for the first time in 1893. The meeting that took place at the Chicago World's Fair joined women from all over the globe with the expressed purpose of defining publicly the changing social needs brought about by industrialization and to legitimate women's visibility in the international arena (Boulding, 1988). A constellation of powerful oil companies were first developing (e.g., the Standard Oil Companies, now EXXON, MOBIL, AMOCO), and union workers and U.S. Steel company executives had their first confrontation in the Homestead strike of 1893 (the union was crushed). These are just a few examples, and your own experiences, goals, and dreams will make other linkages more salient. Nonetheless, each of these events clearly has strong and direct connections with what is going on in organizations today. To understand contemporary organizations, we must embrace our past as well as our future. Our personal lives as well as our organizational lives are sustained and complicated by clusters of connections that we call upon and that call upon us. These linkages embed us in our history.

---

**MAKING CONNECTIONS**

*Anthony N. Judge*, an employee in the Brussels office of the Union of International Associations, eloquently describes the importance of a network perspective for solving today's problems. His words, written in the appendix of *The Yearbook of World Problems and Human Potential* (1976), portend contemporary trends.

"A fundamental difficulty today is the predilection for simplistic hierarchical representation of the interrelationships between concepts, between organizations and between problems. This is so despite the constant exposure to the evidence that these hierarchies do not contain the complexity in which society has to deal.... Neither a hierarchical organization nor a hierarchy of concepts can handle a network of environmental problems, for example, without leaving many dangerous gaps through which unforeseen problems may emerge and be uncontainable" (quoted in Lipnack & Stamps, 1986, pp. 162-163).

## ❏ The Ethical Implications
of the Network Perspective

Another implication of our network metaphor is that organizational communication is not value-free, there is a strong ethical component to our message behavior. A focus on the interconnections between our actions as corporate citizens and our actions as global citizens, the embeddedness of our experiences in and outside organizational contexts, and the permeability of boundaries expand the relevant participants in the organizational conversation. Understanding our connectedness reconstitutes notions of community and home. A fundamental dimension of communicative and organizational competence becomes social responsibility. As individual communicators, we may feel responsible only for what we intend; as members of interlocking and overlapping networks, we become responsible for what we do and say.

> *Understanding our connectedness reconstitutes our notions of community.*

Robert Jackall vividly demonstrates the ethical implications of our embedded relationships in his 1988 classic, *Moral Mazes: The World of Corporate Managers*. From intensive fieldwork in several bureaucratic organizations, he concludes that a typical organization is an intricate maze, a bewildering structure of relationships in which individuals can easily hide and thus escape responsibility for their deeds and utterances. "Bureaucracies," he writes, "may be thought of as vast systems of organized irresponsibility" (p. 127). Ironically, the departmentalized and depersonalized networks of bureaucracy distance individuals from, and desensitize them to, the ethical components of their messages, while at the very same time it is these connections that make communication so powerful.

Thus the ethical and practical implications of our network metaphor are far reaching. Approaching organizations as networks may indeed change the way we interpret, communicate, and imagine the world. Gundren Tempel, a German social scien-

## MAKING CONNECTIONS

Responsible communicators, the eminent organizational communication scholar *W. Charles Redding* (1992) argues, must not only observe high personal moral and ethical standards, they must freely acknowledge authorship of their communicative acts. Responsibility includes a serious concern for the predictable consequences of our communication within our networks and the recognition of our direct connection to what occurs.

In a speech to a group of graduate students studying organizational communication at Purdue University (Spring 1992), Redding classified unethical messages in the following way:

| MESSAGE TYPE | EXAMPLE |
|---|---|
| 1. Abusive/insensitive | insults, harassing comments |
| 2. Deceptive/manipulative/ seductive | false promises, lies, ingratiation |
| 3. Coercive | threats, demands based on disparity of power |
| 4. Secretive | strategic silence |
| 5. Intrusive | hidden surveillance |

Most notably, as the last two message types indicate, Redding (1988) contends that "silence is frequently a communicative act, coequal in impact with voice" (p. 702). He suggests that there are two identifiable forms of silence: *illegitimate listening* and the *absence of messages*.

*Illegitimate listening* includes many forms of wire-tapping, testing, and surveillance of employees. In all these cases, employees unwittingly become involved in communication networks and there is no ownership of the consequences.

*Absence of messages* includes the failure to speak out when injustice ought to be opposed or relevant information is withheld. *Zero messages* constitute the silence when a specific message is expected but not forthcoming. Redding (1990) uses the well-known case of Robbins Company and the Dalkon shield to provide a vivid example of irresponsible silence. For more than 10 years, a clique of top managers remained silent about the documented illnesses and deaths associated with defects in the design of the Dalkon shield. Even when an employee indicated to his manager that he could not, in good conscience, remain silent about the dangerous defects in the product, a supervisor is reported to have replied, "Your conscience does not pay your salary" (p. 15). Not until years later when there was compelling evidence communicated outside the traditional organizational networks to the public at large did the company finally issue an official directive explicitly urging physicians to remove the Dalkon shield from women who were still wearing it.

tist, spent months traveling around the globe with the chief executive officers of several multinational corporations. Her words poignantly reflect the powerful lenses of a network perspective, lenses that are strong enough to bring into focus entire matrices of connections while sensitive enough to detail the individual elements, lenses that give us the responsibility and the potential to create and sustain human organization:

> The very first time I ever sat in a [multinational corporation] chairman's office I imagined what the room would be like if I had worked there. I decided I would cover one wall, the one opposite the desk, with a photograph of people (no matter what nationality, Russians in Red Square, Americans in Laurel Park; just a great mass of faces from end to end), and I would get pictures of all my friends and of my family and put one into each square foot so that whenever my eyes wandered across the wall I would see faces of those I know and love, and be brought back to reality. Whatever I do to two thousand million I do to those familiar faces. What I think of those two thousand million must ultimately be reflected in my thoughts of my friends, however much I may try to keep the two apart. And, somewhere in this great mass of faces on the wall, in some corner, I would have to find my own face. (Tempel, 1970, p. 68)

## ❏ Final Connections

This book focused upon the multileveled interfaces between organizational and interpersonal domains. The network metaphor, chosen to capture these complex linkages, highlighted the richness, significance, and complex nature of organizational communication. Six dynamic aspects of interaction were addressed:

Networks are stable and ever changing.
Networks are collective manifestations of personal choices.
Networks are powerful organizational structures that must be constituted and reconstituted through interpersonal communication.
Network influences evolve from indirect as well as direct connections.

Network memberships foster individuality.
Network interconnectedness stimulates yet constrains innovation
    and change.

A consistent message flowed through the text. Although we cannot actually see or touch these metaphorical networks, they have powerful consequences that go far beyond the workplace. It is through communication that we evolve our culture, our social structures, our worldviews, and shape our perceptions of what is and what could be. A better understanding of organizational communication enables and empowers us to participate in and contribute to our global society.

# References

Acker, J. (1990). Hierarchies, jobs, bodies: A theory of gendered organizations. *Gender & Society, 4*(2), 139-158.

Ackoff, R. (1974). *Redesigning the future: A systems approach to societal problems.* New York: Wiley.

Adams, J. (1983). *Participant observation at the Assistance and Support for Battered Women's Shelter.* Unpublished paper.

Adler, N. (1991). *International dimensions of organizational behavior* (2nd ed.). Boston: PWS Kent.

Albrecht, T. (1979). The role of communication in perceptions of organizational climate. In D. Nimmo (Ed.), *Communication yearbook 3* (pp. 343-357). New Brunswick, NJ: Transaction.

Albrecht, T., & Adelman, M. (1984). Social support and life stress: New directions for communication research. *Human Communication Research, 11*(1), 3-32.

Albrecht, T., & Hall, B. (1991). Facilitating talk about new ideas: The role of personal relationships in organizational innovation. *Communication Monographs, 58*(3), 273-289.

Albrecht, T., & Ropp, V. (1984). Communicating about innovation in networks of three U.S. organizations. *Journal of Communication, 34*(3), 78-91.

Alger, C. (1965). Personal contact in intergovernmental organizations. In H. Kelman (Ed.), *International behavior* (pp. 521-547). New York: Holt, Rinehart & Winston.

*American Heritage Dictionary of the American Language.* (1978). Boston: Houghton Mifflin.

175

Ancona, D., & Caldwell, D. (1988). Beyond task and maintenance: Defining external functions in groups. *Group & Organization Studies, 13*(4), 468-494.

Axley, S. (1984). Managerial and organizational communication in terms of the conduit metaphor. *Academy of Management Review, 9,* 428-437.

Banks, A., & Metzgar, J. (1989). *Participating in management: Union organizing on a new terrain.* Chicago: Midwest Center for Labor Research.

Barker, J. (1993). Tightening the iron cage: Concertive control in self-managing teams. *Administrative Science Quarterly, 38,* 408-437.

Barnard, C. (1968). *The functions of the executive.* Cambridge, MA: Harvard University Press. (Original work published 1938)

Barringer, F. (1992, March 21). Couples with 2 jobs ask when interests conflict. *New York Times,* p. 6.

Bartlett, J. (1983). *Success and failure in quality circles: A study of 25 companies.* Cambridge: Crown.

Bateson, G. (1972). *Steps to an ecology of mind.* New York: Ballantine.

Baumgartner, M. (1988). *The moral order of a suburb.* New York: Oxford University Press.

Bavelas, A. (1950). Communication patterns in task-oriented groups. *Acoustical Society of America Journal, 22,* 727-730.

Bell, R., Roloff, M., VanCamp, K., & Karsol, S. (1990). Is it lonely at the top? Career success and personal relationships. *Journal of Communication, 4*(1), 9-23.

Bellah, R., Madsen, R., Sullivan, W., Swidler, A., & Tipton, S. (1985). *Habits of the heart: Individualism and commitment in American life.* Berkeley: University of California Press.

Berge, M. (1987, July/August). Building bridges over the cultural rivers. *International Management, 42*(5), 61-62.

Better, N. M. (1991, December 8). Image-making, from soup to sales pitch. *New York Times,* p. 29.

Bingham, S., & Burleson, B. (1989). Multiple effects of messages with multiple goals: Some perceived outcomes of responses to sexual harassment. *Human Communication Research, 16,* 184-216.

Black, J., & Stephens, G. (1989). The influence of the spouse on American expatriate adjustment and intent to stay in Pacific overseas assignments. *Journal of Management, 5*(4), 529-544.

Blake, R., & Mouton, J. (1964). *The managerial grid.* Houston: Gulf.

Blau, J., & Alba, R. (1982). Empowering nets of participation. *Administrative Science Quarterly, 27,* 363-379.

Block that metaphor. (1987, December 28). *The New Yorker,* p. 50.

Boje, D. (1991). The storytelling organization: A study of story performance in an office supply firm. *Administrative Science Quarterly, 36,* 106-126.

Bond, M., & Hwang, K. (1986). The social psychology of Chinese people. In M. Bond (Ed.), *The psychology of the Chinese people* (pp. 213-266). Hong Kong: Oxford University Press.

Bott, E. (1957). *Family and social networks.* London: Tavistock.

Boulding, E. (1988). *Building a global civic culture: Education for an interdependent world.* New York: Teachers College Press.

Brandt, B. (1990, October). If we just had more time. *Dollars & Sense, 160,* 16-18.

Brass, D. (1984). Being in the right place: A structural analysis of individual influence in an organization. *Administrative Science Quarterly, 29,* 518-539.

Brass, D. (1985). Men and women's networks. *Academy of Management Journal, 2,* 327-343.

Brown, R., & Levinson, S. (1978). Universals in language usage: Politeness phenomena. In E. Goody (Ed.), *Questions and politeness* (pp. 56-89). Cambridge: Cambridge University Press.

Bureau of National Affairs, Inc. (1988). Sexual harassment among civil servants. *Fair Employment Practices, 7,* 82.

Burke, K. (1969). *A rhetoric of motives.* Berkeley: University of California Press. (Original work published 1950)

Burt, R. (1983). Cohesion versus structural equivalence as a basis for network subgroups. In R. Burt & M. Minor (Eds.), *Applied network analysis.* Beverly Hills, CA: Sage.

Bylinski, G. (1990, July 2). Turning R&D into real products. *Fortune,* pp. 52-60.

Caplan, G. (1976). The family as a support system. In G. Caplan & M. Killilea (Eds.), *Support systems and mutual help* (pp. 19-36). New York: Grune & Stratton.

Carnegie, D. (1981). *How to win friends and influence people.* New York: Simon & Schuster.

CEO survey. (1992, July-August). *Across the Board,* pp. 9-11.

Chang, H., & Holt, G. (1991). More than relationship: Chinese interaction and the principle of kuan-hsi. *Communication Quarterly, 39(3),* 251-271.

Cheney, G. (1983). The rhetoric of identification and the study of organizational communication. *Quarterly Journal of Speech, 69,* 143-158.

Cheney, G. (1991). *Rhetoric in an organizational society.* Columbia: University of South Carolina Press.

Cheney, G. (1995). Democracy in the workplace: Theory and practice from the perspective of communication. *Journal of Applied Communication Research, 23,* 1-34.

Clair, R. (1993). The use of framing devices to sequester organizational narratives: Hegemony and harassment. *Communication Monographs, 60,* 113-136.

Clair, R., McGoun, M., & Spirek, M. (1993). Sexual harassment responses of working women: An assessment of current communication oriented typologies and perceived effectiveness of the response. In G. Kreps (Ed.), *Sexual harassment: Communication implications* (pp. 200-224). Creskill, NJ: Hampton.

Clegg, S. (1990). *Modern organizations: Organization studies in the postmodern world.* London: Sage.

Cleveland, H. (1985, January-February). The twilight of hierarchy: Speculations on the global information society. *Public Administration Review,* pp. 185-195.

Cobb, S. (1976). Social support as a moderator of life stress. *Psychosomatic Medicine, 38,* 300-314.

Cockburn, C. (1991). *In the way of women.* Ithaca, NY: ILR Press.

Contractor, N., Eisenberg, E., & Monge, P. (1992). *Antecedents and outcomes of interpretive diversity in organizations.* Unpublished manuscript.

Cooley, C. (1902). *Human nature and the social order.* New York: Scribner.

Cooper, R., & Fox, S. (1990). The "texture" of organizing. *Journal of Management Studies, 27(6),* 575-582.

Dahl, R. (1961). *Who governs?* New Haven, CT: Yale University Press.

Daniels, T., & Logan, L. (1983). Communication in women's career development relationships. In R. N. Bostrom (Ed.), *Communication yearbook 7* (pp. 532-553). Beverly Hills, CA: Sage.

Danowski, J. (1980). Group attitude uniformity and connectivity of organizational communication networks for production, innovation and maintenance content. *Human Communication Research, 6,* 299-308.

Davis, M. (1982). *Families in a working world.* New York: Praeger.

Deal, T., & Kennedy, A. (1982). *Corporate cultures: The rights and rituals of corporate life.* Reading, MA: Addison-Wesley.

Deetz, S. (1992). *Democracy in an age of corporate colonization: Developments in communication and the politics of everyday life.* Albany: State University of New York Press.

DeMente, B. (1981). *The Japanese way of doing business: The psychology of management in Japan.* Englewood Cliffs, NJ: Prentice Hall.

de Tocqueville, A. (1945). *Democracy in America.* New York: Alfred Knopf. (Original work published in 1840)

Dillard, J. (1987). Close relationships at work: Perceptions of the motives and performance of relational participants. *Journal of Social and Personal Relationships, 4,* 179-183.

Driessnack, C. (1987, August). Spouse relocation: A moving experience. *Personnel Administrator,* pp. 95-103.

Dun & Bradstreet. (1992). *Million dollar directory* (Vol. 2). New York: Author.

Duncan, W., Smeltzer, L., & Leap, T. (1990). Humor and work: Applications of joking behavior to management. *Journal of Management, 16*(2), 255-278.

Edwards, R. (1979). *Contested terrain: The transformation of the workplace in the twentieth century.* New York: Basic Books.

Edwards, R. (1981). The social relations of production at the point of production. In M. Zey-Ferrel & M. Aiken (Eds.), *Complex organizations: Critical perspectives* (pp. 152-182). Glenview, IL: Scott, Foresman.

Ehrenrich, B. (1989). *Fear of falling: The inner life of the middle class.* New York: Pantheon.

Eisenberg, E. (1984). Ambiguity as strategy in organizational communication. *Communication Monographs, 51,* 227-242.

Eisenberg, E., Monge, P., & Miller, K. (1983). Involvement in communication networks as a predictor of organizational commitment. *Human Communication Research, 10,* 179-201.

Etheridge, L. (1985). *Can governments learn? American foreign policy and Central American revolutions.* New York: Pergamon.

Fagenson, E. (1988). The power of a mentor. *Group & Organizational Studies, 13*(2), 182-184.

Fairhurst, G. (1986). Male-female communication on the job: Literature review and commentary. In M. McLaughlin (Ed.), *Communication yearbook 9* (pp. 83-116). Beverly Hills, CA: Sage.

Fairhurst, G., Green, S., & Snavely, B. (1984). Face support in controlling poor performance. *Human Communication Research, 11,* 272-295.

Fairhurst, G., Rogers, L., & Sarr, R. (1987). Manager-subordinate control patterns and judgments about the relationship. In M. McLaughlin (Ed.), *Communication yearbook 10* (pp. 395-415). Newbury Park, CA: Sage.

Farace, V., Monge, P., & Russell, H. (1977). *Communicating and organizing.* Reading, MA: Addison-Wesley.

Fayol, H. (1925). *General industrial management* (C. Storrs, Trans.). London: Pitman.

Feldman, D. (1988). *Managing careers in organizations.* Glenview IL: Scott, Foresman.

Ferree, M. (1987). Equality and autonomy. In M. Katzenstein & C. Mudler (Eds.), *The women's movements of the United States and Western Europe* (pp. 39-52). Philadelphia: Temple University Press.

Finder, J. (1987, February 22). A male secretary. *New York Times Magazine*, p. 68.

Finder, J. (1992, April 12). Ultimate insider, ultimate outsider. *New York Times Book Review*, pp. 1, 25-27.

Fine, G. (1986). Friendships in the workplace. In V. Derlega & B. Winstead (Eds.), *Friendship and social interaction* (pp. 185-206). New York: Springer-Verlag.

Fisher, C., Ilgen, D., & Troyer, W. (1979). Source credibility, information favorability, and job offer acceptance. *Academy of Management Journal, 22*, 94-103.

Folger, J., & Poole, M. (1984). *Working through conflict.* Glenview, IL: Scott, Foresman.

Follett, M. (1941). Constructive conflict. In H. Metcalf & L. Urwick (Eds.), *Dynamic administration: The collected papers of Mary Parker Follet* (pp. 30-49). New York: Harper.

Franke, R., & Kaul, J. (1978). The Hawthorne experiments: First statistical reinterpretation. *American Sociological Review, 43*, 623-643.

Fuchsberg, G. (1990, April 27-28). Blessed are they who sit by thrones of corporate gods. *Wall Street Journal*, pp. 1, 7.

Galaskiewicz, J., & Wasserman, S. (1989). Mimetic processes within an interorganizational field: An empirical test. *Administrative Science Quarterly, 34*, 454-479.

Gamson, Z., & Levin, H. (1984). Obstacles to the survival of democratic workplaces. In R. Jackall & H. Levin (Eds.), *Worker cooperatives in America* (pp. 219-244). Berkeley: University of California Press.

Gillette, E. (1987, February 4). Higher education's caste system: Injustice is a daily experience. *Chronicle of Higher Education*, p. 96.

Gladstein-Ancona, D., & Caldwell, D. (1987). Management issues facing new product teams in high technology companies. *Advances in Industrial and Labor Relations, 4*, 199-221.

Glickman, N., & Woodward, D. (1989). *The new competitors: How foreign investors are changing the U.S. economy.* New York: Basic Books.

Goffman, E. (1967). *Interaction ritual.* Garden City, NY: Anchor.

Gottfried, H., & Weiss, P. (1994). Unsettling boundaries: A compound feminist organization: Purdue University's Council on the Status of Women. *Women and Politics, 14*, 2.

Gould, M. (1979). When women create an organization: The ideological imperatives of feminism. In D. Dunkerlay & G. Solomon (Eds.), *The international yearbook of women's studies.* London: Routledge & Kegan Paul.

Grabosky, P., & Braithwaite, J. (1986). *Of manners gentle: Enforcement strategies of Australian business regulatory agencies.* Melbourne, Australia: Oxford University Press.

Granovetter, M. (1974). *Getting a job: A study of contacts and careers.* Cambridge, MA: Harvard University Press.

Granovetter, M. (1983). The strength of weak ties: Network theory revisited. In R. Collins (Ed.), *Sociological theory* (pp. 201-233). San Francisco: Jossey-Bass.

Granovetter, M. (1985). Economic action and social structure: The problem of embeddedness. *American Journal of Sociology, 91*(3), 481-510.

Grauerholz, E., & Koralewiski, M. (Eds.). (1991). *Sexual coercion: A sourcebook on its nature, causes, and prevention.* Lexington, MA: Lexington.

Greenberg, E. (1986). *Workplace democracy: The political effects of participation.* Ithaca, NY: Cornell University Press.

Grenier, G. (1988). *Inhuman relations: Quality circles and anti-unionism in American industry.* Philadelphia: Temple University Press.

Gudykunst, W. (1991). *Bridging differences: Effective intergroup communication.* Newbury Park, CA: Sage.

Guetzkow, H. (1965). Communication in organizations. In J. March (Ed.), *Handbook of organizations* (pp. 534-573). Chicago: Rand McNally.

Gulliver, P. (1979). *Disputes and negotiations: A cross-cultural perspective.* New York: Academic Press.

Gutek, B., & Morasch, B. (1982). Sex ratios, sex-role spillover and sexual harassment at work. *Journal of Social Issues, 38*(4), 55-74.

Guterl, F. (1989, February). Goodbye, old matrix. *Dun's Business Month,* pp. 32-38.

Hall, D., & Richter, J. (1990). Career gridlock: Baby boomers hit the wall. *The Executive, 10*(3), 7-22.

Hall, E. (1980). *The silent language.* Westport, CT: Greenwood.

Hall, E., & Hall, M. (1989). *Understanding cultural differences.* Yarmouth, ME: Intercultural Press.

Hammer, M., & Champy, J. (1993). *Reengineering the corporation: A manifesto for business revolution.* New York: HarperBusiness.

Hampden-Turner, C., & Trompenaars, F. (1993). *The seven cultures of capitalism.* New York: Doubleday.

Harvey, J. (1989). Some thoughts about organizational backstabbing: Or, how come every time I get stabbed in the back my fingerprints are on the knife? *Academy of Management Executive, 111*(4), 271-277.

Hearn, J., & Parkin, P. (1987). *"Sex" at "work": The power and paradox of organization sexuality.* Brighton, UK: Wheatsheaf.

Heide, J. (1992). The shadow of the future: Effects of anticipated interaction and frequency of contact on buyer-seller cooperation. *Academy of Management Journal, 35,* 265-291.

Hiroshi, K. (1991). Death and the corporate warrior. *Japan Quarterly, 39,* 149-157.

Hirsch, B. (1979). Psychological dimensions of social networks: A multi-method analysis. *American Journal of Community Psychology, 7,* 263-277.

Hirsch, J. (1990, February 26). Older workers chafe under young managers. *Wall Street Journal,* pp. B1, B6.

Hirschman, E. (1981). Social and cognitive influences on information exposure. *Journal of Communication, 31*(1), 76-87.

Hochschild, A. (1989). *The second shift: Working parents and the revolution at home.* New York: Viking.

Hofstede, G. (1984). *Culture's consequences.* London: Sage.

Hollander, E. (1958). Conformity, status, and idiosyncracy credit. *Psychological Review, 65,* 117-127.

Horn, P., & Horn, J. (1982). *Sex in the office: Power and passion in the workplace.* Reading, MA: Addison-Wesley.

House, R. (1981). *Work stress and social support*. Reading, MA: Addison-Wesley.

Howard, R. (1986). *Brave new workplace*. New York: Penguin.

How 21 men got global in 35 days. (1989, November 6). *Fortune*, pp. 71-79.

Hu, W., & Grove, C. (1991). *Encountering the Chinese: A guide for Americans.* Yarmouth, ME: Intercultural Press.

Jablin, F. (1979). Superior-subordinate communication: The state of the art. *Psychological Bulletin, 86*, 1201-1222.

Jablin, F. (1987). Organizational entry, assimilation, and exit. In F. Jablin, L. Putnam, K. Roberts, & L. Porter (Eds.), *Handbook of organizational communication: An interdisciplinary approach* (pp. 679-740). Newbury Park, CA: Sage.

Jablin, F., & Sussman, L. (1983). Organizational group communication: A review of literature and model of the process. In H. H. Greenbaum, R. Falcione, & S. Hellweg (Eds.), *Organizational communication: Abstracts, analysis, and overview* (Vol. 8, pp. 11-50). Beverly Hills, CA: Sage.

Jackall, R. (1988). *Moral mazes: The world of corporate managers*. New York: Oxford University Press.

Jackson, S. (Ed.). (1992). *Diversity in the workplace: Human resource initiatives*. New York: Guilford.

Janis, I. (1989). *Crucial decisions: Leadership in policy making and crisis management*. New York: Free Press.

Jermier, J. (1988). Sabotage at work. The rational view. In S. Bacharach & N. DiTomaso (Eds.), *Research in the sociology of organizations* (pp. 131-149). Greenwich, CT: JAI.

Johnston, W., & Packer, A. (1987). *Workforce 2000: Work and workers for the 21st century*. Indianapolis, IN: Hudson Institute.

Judge, A. (1976). Appendix. In *Yearbook of world problems and human potential* (pp. 842-844). Brussels: Secretariats of Union of International Associations.

Kadushin, C. (1978). Small world: How many steps to the top? *Detroit News, 106*(26), A19.

Kahn, R., Wolfe, D., Quinn, R., & Snoek, D., in collaboration with Rosenthal, R. (1964). *Organizational stress*. New York: Wiley.

Kanter, R. (1977). *Work and family in the United States: A critical review and agenda for research and policy*. New York: Russell Sage.

Kanter, R. (1983). *The changemasters: Innovation and entrepreneurship in the American corporation*. New York: Simon & Schuster.

Katz, D., & Kahn, R. (1966). *The social psychology of organizations*. New York: Wiley.

Kidder, T. (1981). *The soul of a new machine*. Boston: Little, Brown.

Kiechel, W. (1989, April 10). The workaholic generation. *Fortune*, pp. 50-62.

Killworth, P., & Bernard, H. (1976). Informant accuracy in social network data. *Human Organization, 3*, 269-286.

Kipnis, D., & Schmidt, S. (1982). *Profile of organizational influence strategies*. San Diego, CA: University Associates.

Kipnis, D., & Schmidt, S. (1985, April). The language of persuasion. *Psychology Today*, pp. 40-48.

Kluckhohn, F., & Strodtbeck, F. (1961). *Variations in value orientations*. New York: Harper & Row.

Knapp, M. (1984). *Interpersonal communication and human relationships*. Newton, MA: Allyn & Bacon.

Knoke, D., & Wood, J. (1981). *Organized for action: Commitment in voluntary associations.* New Brunswick, NJ: Rutgers University Press.

Kras, E. (1988). *Management in two cultures: Bridging the gap between U.S. and Mexican managers.* Yarmouth, ME: Intercultural Press.

Kraut, A., Pedigo, P., McKenna, D., & Dunnette, M. (1989). The role of the manager: What's really important in different management jobs. *Academy of Management Executive, 3*(4), 286-293.

Krone, K., Jablin, F., & Putnam, L. (1987). Communication theory and organizational communication: Multiple perspectives. In F. Jablin, L. Putnam, K. Roberts, & L. Porter (Eds.), *Handbook of organizational communication: An interdisciplinary approach* (pp. 18-40). Newbury Park, CA: Sage.

Labich, K. (1988, June 6). *Fortune,* p. 53.

Laing, R. (1970). *Knots.* New York: Pantheon.

Lakoff, G., & Johnson, M. (1980). *Metaphors we live by.* Chicago: University of Chicago Press.

Lane, H., & DiStefano, J. (1988). *International management behavior.* Toronto, Canada: Nelson.

Lawler, E. (1986). *High involvement management: Participative strategies for improving organizational performance.* San Francisco: Jossey-Bass.

Leavitt, H. (1951). Some effects of certain communication patterns on group performance. *American Journal of Sociology, 46,* 38-50.

Likert, R. (1961). *New patterns of management.* New York: McGraw-Hill.

Lincoln, J., & Miller, J. (1979). Work and friendship ties in organizations: A comparative analysis of relational networks. *Administrative Science Quarterly, 24,* 181-199.

Lindenfeld, F., & Rothschild-Whitt, J. (Eds.). (1982). *Workplace democracy and social change.* Boston: Porter Sargent.

Lipnack, J., & Stamps, J. (1986). *The networking book: People connecting with people.* London: Routledge & Kegan Paul.

Lipton, F., Cohen, C., Fischer, E., & Katz, S. (1981). Schizophrenia: A network crisis. *Schizophrenia Bulletin, 7,* 144-151.

Livingston, J. (1982). Responses to sexual harassment on the job: Legal, organizational, and individual actions. *Journal of Social Issues, 38*(4), 5-22.

Macaulay, S. (1963). Non-contractual relations in business. *American Sociological Review, 28,* 55-70.

MacKinnon, C. (1979). *Sexual harassment of working women.* New Haven, CT: Yale University Press.

Marshall, J. (1989). Re-visioning career concepts: A feminist invitation. In M. Archer, T. Hall, & B. Lawrence (Eds.), *Handbook of career theory* (pp. 275-291). Cambridge, UK: Cambridge University Press.

Martin, J., Feldman, M., Hatch, M., & Sethin, S. (1983). The uniqueness paradox in organizational stories. *Administrative Science Quarterly, 28,* 438-453.

Martin, J., & Meyerson, D. (1988). Organizational cultures and the denial, channeling, and acknowledging of ambiguity. In L. Pondy, R. Boland, & H. Thomas (Eds.), *Managing ambiguity and change* (pp. 93-125). New York: Wiley.

Mayo, E. (1960). *The human problems of industrial civilization.* New York: Viking. (Original work published 1933)

McPhee, R. (1986). A model of social network development in organizations. *Central States Speech Journal, 37*(1), 8-18.

Mechanic, D. (1962). Sources of power and lower participants in complex organizations. *Administrative Science Quarterly, 7*, 349-364.

Merrill, H. (Ed.). (1960). *Classics in management.* New York: American Management Association.

Michels, R. (1962). *Political parties: A sociological study of the oligarchical tendencies of modern democracy.* New York: Free Press.

Milgram, S. (1967). The small world problem. *Psychology Today, 1*, 61-67.

Miller, K., Ellis, B., Zook, E., & Lyles, J. (1990). An integrated model of communication, stress, and burnout in the workplace. *Communication Research, 17*, 300-326.

Miller, K., & Monge, P. (1986). Participation, satisfaction, and productivity: A meta-analytic review. *Academy of Management Journal, 29*, 727-753.

Mills, C. (1957). *The power elite.* New York: Oxford University Press.

Milroy, L., & Margrain, S. (1980). Vernacular language loyalty and social networks. *Language in Society, 9*(1), 43-70.

Mitchell, R. (1979). *Less than words can say.* Boston: Little, Brown.

Mitroff, T. (1987). *Business NOT as usual.* San Francisco: Jossey-Bass.

Monge, P., & Eisenberg, E. (1987). Emergent communication networks. In F. Jablin, L. Putnam, K. Roberts, & L. Porter (Eds.), *Handbook of organizational communication: An interdisciplinary perspective* (pp. 304-342). Newbury Park, CA: Sage.

Morgan, G. (1986). *Images of organization.* Newbury Park, CA: Sage.

Morrill, C. (1991). The customs of conflict management among corporate executives. *American Anthropologist, 93*(4), 871-892.

Mulgan, G. (1991). *Communication and control: Networks and the new economies of communication.* New York: Guilford.

Mumby, D. (1987). The political function of narrative in organizations. *Communication Monographs, 54*, 113-127.

Mumby, D. (1988). *Communication and power in organizations: Discourse, ideology and domination.* Norwood, NJ: Ablex.

Mumby, D., & Putnam, L. (1992). The politics of emotion: A feminist reading of bounded rationality. *Academy of Management Review, 17*(3), 465-486.

Mumby, D., & Stohl, C. (1991). Power and discourse in organization studies: Absence and the dialectic of control. *Discourse & Society, 2*, 313-332.

Naisbitt, J., & Aburdene, P. (1990). *Megatrends 2000: Ten new directions for the 1990's.* New York: Morrow.

Neugarten, D., & Shafritz, J. (1980). *Sexuality in organizations: Romantic and coercive behaviors at work.* Oak Park, IL: Moore.

Pacanowsky, M. (1988). Communication in the empowering organization. In J. Anderson (Ed.), *Communication yearbook 11* (pp. 264-277). Newbury Park, CA: Sage.

Pandey, J. (1986). Attribution and evaluation of manipulative behavior. *Journal of Social Psychology, 126*, 735-744.

Parker, M., & Slaughter, J. (1988). *Choosing sides: Unions and the team concept.* Boston: South End.

Parsons, T. (1951). *The social system.* New York: Free Press.

Pateman, C. (1970). *Participation and democratic theory.* Cambridge: Cambridge University Press.

Pearce, M., & David, J. (1983). A social network approach to organizational design-performance. *Academy of Management Journal, 26*(3), 436-444.

Pelz, D. (1952). Influence: A key to effective leadership in the first-line supervisor. *Personnel, 29,* 3-11.

Perrucci, R., Anderson, R., Schendel, D., & Trachtman, L. (1980). Whistle-blowing: Professionals' resistance to organizational authority. *Social Problems, 28,* 149-164.

Perrucci, R., & Pilisuk, M. (1970). Leaders and ruling elites: The interorganizational bases of community power. *American Sociological Review, 35,* 1040-1057.

Peters, T., & Waterman, R. (1982). *In search of excellence.* New York: Harper & Row.

Poll finds women's gains have taken personal toll. (1989, August 29). *New York Times,* pp. 1, 8.

Putnam, L. (1985). Contradictions and paradoxes in organizations. In L. Thayer (Ed.), *Organization communication: Emerging perspectives* (Vol. 1, pp. 151-157). Norwood, NJ: Ablex.

Putnam, L. (1989). Perspectives for research on group embeddedness in organizations. In S. King (Ed.), *Human communication as a field of study* (pp. 163-180). Albany: State University of New York Press.

Putnam, L., & Poole, M. (1987). Conflict and negotiation. In F. Jablin, L. Putnam, K. Roberts, & L. Porter (Eds.), *Handbook of organizational communication: An interdisciplinary perspective* (pp. 549-599). Newbury Park, CA: Sage.

Putnam, L., & Stohl, C. (1990). Bona fide groups: A reconceptualization of groups in context. *Communication Studies, 41*(3), 248-265.

Putnam, L., & Wilson, C. (1982). Communicative strategies in organizational conflicts: Reliability and validity of a measurement scale. In M. Burgoon (Ed.), *Communication yearbook 6* (pp. 629-652). Beverly Hills, CA: Sage.

Quinn, R. (1980). Coping with Cupid: The formation, impact, and management of romantic relationships in organizations. In D. Neugarten & J. Shafritz (Eds.), *Sexuality in organizations: Romantic and coercive behaviors at work* (pp. 38-52). Oak Park, IL: Moore.

Rapp, E. (1992, February). Dangerous liaisons. *Working Woman,* pp. 56-61.

Rawlins, W. (1992). *Friendship matters: Communication, dialectics, and the life course.* Hawthorne, NY: Aldine de Gruyter.

Ray, E. B. (1987). Support relationships and occupational stress in the workplace. In T. Albrecht, M. Adelman, & Associates, *Communicating social support* (pp. 172-191). Newbury Park, CA: Sage.

Ray, E. B. (1993). When the links become chains: Considering dysfunctions of supportive communication in the workplace. *Communication Monographs, 60*(1), 106-111.

Ray, E. B., & Miller, K. (1991). The influence of communication structure and social support on job stress and burnout. *Management Communication Quarterly, 4*(4), 506-527.

Redding, W. C. (1972). *Communication within the organization: An interpretive review of theory and research.* New York: Industrial Communication Council.

Redding, W. C. (1988). The enemies of responsible communication. *Vital Speeches, 54*(22), 702-704.

Redding, W. C. (1990, June). *Ethics and the study of organizational communication: A case of culpable neglect.* Paper presented at the SCA Conference on Ethics in Communication, Gull Lake, MI.

Redding, W. C. (1992, April 19). *Ethical issues of organizational communication.* Lecture presented at Purdue University, West Lafayette, IN.

Reynolds, E., & Johnson, J. (1982). Liaison emergence: Relating theoretical perspectives. *Academy of Management Review, 7,* 551-559.

Richmond, V., Davis, L., Saylor, K., & McCroskey, J. (1984). Power strategies in organizations: Communication techniques and messages. *Human Communication Research, 11,* 85-108.

Roberts, K., & O'Reilly, C. (1979). Some correlates of communication roles in organizations. *Academy of Management Journal, 22,* 42-57.

Roethlisberger, F., & Dickson, W. (1939). *Management and the worker.* New York: Wiley.

Rogers, E., & Agarwala-Rogers, R. (1976). *Communication in organizations.* New York: Free Press.

Rogers, E., & Farace, R. (1975). Relational communication analysis: New measures and procedures. *Human Communication Research, 1,* 222-239.

Rogers, E., & Kincaid, D. (1981). *Communication networks: Toward a new paradigm for research.* New York: Free Press.

Rosen, C., Klein, K., & Young, K. (1986). *Employee ownership in America.* Lexington, MA: Lexington.

Rosenberg, R. (1985, February). Utopia, Inc. *Inc.,* pp. 52-60.

Rosnow, R., & Fine, G. (1976). *Rumor and gossip: The social psychology of hearsay.* New York: Elsevier.

Sanger, D. E. (1992, April 23). Unusual path to the top at Mitsubishi. *New York Times,* Business Day section, pp. C1, C3.

Sashkin, M. (1984). Participative management is an ethical imperative. *Organizational Dynamics, 12,* 5-22.

Scardino, A. (1988, January 18). Young name dropper wins riches and a date in court. *New York Times,* p. 8.

Schiappa, E. (1989). "Spheres of Argument" as *topoi* for the critical study of power/knowledge. In B. Gronbeck (Ed.), *Spheres of argument: Proceedings of the Sixth SCA/AFA Conference on Argumentation* (pp. 47-56). Annandale, VA: Speech Communication Association.

Schrank, R. (1978). *Ten thousand working days.* Cambridge: MIT Press.

Scott, W., & Hart, D. (1979). *Organizational America.* Boston: Houghton Mifflin.

Seabright, M., Leventhal, D., & Fichman, M. (1992). Role of individual attachments in the dissolution of interorganizational relationships. *Academy of Management Journal, 35*(1), 122-160.

The secret wars of the CIA. (1987, October 5). *Newsweek,* pp. 41-52.

Shaw, M. (1954). Communication networks. In L. Berkowitz (Ed.), *Advances in experimental psychology* (Vol. 1, pp. 111-147). New York: Academic Press.

The short run. (1990, January-February). *Dollars & Sense, 153,* p. 4.

Shotland, R. (1976). *University communication networks: The small world method.* New York: Wiley.

Sitkin, S. (1989). Secrecy norms in organizational settings. In L. Browning (Ed.), *Conceptual frontiers in organizational communication* (pp. 106-124). White Plains, NY: Longview.

Sitkin, S., & Roth, N. (1993). Explaining the limited effectiveness of legalistic "remedies" for trust/distrust. *Organization Science, 4,* 367-392.

Smircich, L., & Morgan, G. (1982). Leadership: The management of meaning. *Journal of Applied Behavioral Science, 18*(3), 257-273.

Smith, F. (1984). *You and your network.* Waco, TX: Key Word Books.

Smith, R. (1993, May). *Images of organizational communication: Root metaphors of the organization-communication relation*. Paper presented at the International Communication Association convention, Washington, DC.

Soelberg, P. (1967). Unprogrammed decision making. *Industrial Management Review, 8*, 19-27.

Springen, K. (1991, December 16). Retailers with a cause. *Newsweek*, p. 51.

Stohl, C. (1986a). The role of memorable messages in the process of organizational socialization. *Communication Quarterly, 34*, 231-249.

Stohl, C. (1986b). Bridging the parallel organization: A study of quality circle effectiveness. In M. McLaughlin (Ed.), *Communication yearbook 10* (pp. 473-496). Newbury Park, CA: Sage.

Stohl, C. (1989a). Childhood communication networks. In J. Nussbaum (Ed.), *Lifespan communication* (pp. 53-78). Hillsdale, NJ: Lawrence Erlbaum.

Stohl, C. (1989b). Understanding quality circles: A communicative network perspective. In B. Dervin, L. Grossberg, B. O'Keefe, & E. Wartella (Eds.), *Rethinking communication: Vol. 2. Paradigm exemplars* (pp. 346-360). Newbury Park, CA: Sage.

Stohl, C., & Redding, W. (1987). Messages and message exchange processes. In F. Jablin, L. Putnam, K. Roberts, & L. Porter (Eds.), *Handbook of organizational communication: An interdisciplinary approach* (pp. 451-502). Newbury Park, CA: Sage.

Stohl, C., & Sotirin, P. (1990). Absence as workplace control: A critical inquiry. In J. Andersen (Ed.), *Communication yearbook 13* (pp. 59-68). Newbury Park, CA: Sage.

Strauss, G., & Rosenstein, E. (1970). Workers' participation: A critical view. *Industrial Relations, 9*, 197-214.

Sullivan, J. (1981). Family support systems paychecks can't buy. *Family Relations, 30*(3), 607-613.

Taylor, F. (1947). *Principles of scientific management*. New York: Harper. (Original work published 1911)

Taylor, J., & Van Every, E. (1993). *The vulnerable fortress: Bureaucratic organization and management in the information age*. Toronto, Canada: University of Toronto Press.

Tempel, G. (1970). *The chairmen as god*. London: Blond.

Tesser, A., & Rosen, S. (1975). The reluctance to transmit bad news. In I. Berkowitz (Ed.), *Advances in experimental social psychology* (Vol. 8, pp. 193-232). New York: Academic Press.

Thornburg, L. (1990, September). Transfers need not mean dislocation. *Human Resources Magazine*, pp. 46-48.

Tichy, N. (1981). Networks in organizations. In P. Nystrom & W. Starbuck (Eds.), *Handbook of organizational design* (Vol. 2, pp. 203-224). New York: Oxford University Press.

Tirkkonen-Condit, S. (1988, August). *Explicitness vs. implicitness of argumentation: An intercultural comparison*. Paper presented at the Colloquium on the Role of Argument in the Creation of Community, Venice.

Tolsdorf, C. (1976). Social networks, support, and coping: An exploratory study. *Family Process, 15*, 407-417.

Tompkins, P. (1962). *An analysis of communication between headquarters and selected units of a national labor union*. Unpublished dissertation, Purdue University, Lafayette, IN.

Tompkins, P. (1987). Translating organizational theory: Symbolism over substance. In F. Jablin, L. Putnam, K. Roberts, & L. Porter (Eds.), *Handbook of organizational communication: An interdisciplinary approach* (pp. 70-96). Newbury Park, CA: Sage.

Tompkins, P., & Cheney, G. (1985). Communication and unobtrusive control in contemporary organizations. In R. McPhee & P. Tompkins (Eds.), *Organizational communication: Traditional themes and new directions* (pp. 179-210). Beverly Hills, CA: Sage.

Tompkins, P., Fisher, J., Infante, D., & Tompkins, E. (1975). Kenneth Burke and the inherent characteristics of formal organizations: A field study. *Speech Monographs, 42,* 135-142.

Trist, E. (1963). *Organizational choice: Capabilities of groups at the coal factory under changing technologies: The loss, rediscovery, and transformation of a work tradition.* London: Tavistock.

Tubbs, W. (1993) Karoshi: Stress death and the meaning of work. *Journal of Business Ethics, 12,* 869-877.

Tucker, T. (1987). *Fighting it out with difficult—if not impossible—people.* Dubuque, IA: Kendall Hunt.

Tushman, M., & Scanlan, T. (1981). Boundary spanning individuals: Their role in information transfer and their antecedents. *Academy of Management Journal, 24,* 289-305.

The Tylenol scare. (1982, October 11). *Newsweek,* pp. 32-35.

United Press International. (1990, January 30). Avianca crash study continues. *Purdue Exponent,* p. 9.

Van de Ven, A., Emmett, D., & Koenig, R. (1980). Frameworks for interorganizational analyses. In A. R. Negandhi (Ed.), *Interorganizational theory* (pp. 19-38). Kent, OH: Kent State University Press.

Van Maanen, J., & Barley, S. (1984). Occupational communities: Culture and control in organizations. In B. Staw & L. Cummings (Eds.), *Research in Organizational Behavior, 6,* 287-365.

Victor, D. (1992). *International business communication.* New York: HarperCollins.

Voydanoff, P. (Ed.). (1984). *Work and family: Changing roles of men and women.* Palo Alto, CA: Mayfield.

Walters, B. (1986, June 29). Television tactics: Backstage with the Duvaliers. *New York Times,* pp. 1, 15H.

Watzlawick, P., Beavin, J., & Jackson, D. (1967). *Pragmatics of human communication.* New York: Norton.

Weber, M. (1947). *The theory of social and economic organization* (Talcott Parsons & A. Henderson, Trans. & Eds.). New York: Free Press.

Weick, K. (1979). *The social psychology of organizing.* Reading, MA: Addison-Wesley.

Weick, K. (1984). Small wins: Redefining the scale of social problems. *American Psychologist, 39,* 40-49.

Weick, K. (1987). Theorizing about organizational communication. In F. Jablin, L. Putnam, K. Roberts, & L. Porter (Eds.), *Handbook of organizational communication: An interdisciplinary approach* (pp. 97-122). Newbury Park, CA: Sage.

Whyte, W. (1952). *Is anybody listening?* New York: Simon & Schuster.

Whyte, W. (1956). *The organization man.* New York: Simon & Schuster.

Whyte, W., & Whyte, K. (1991). *Making Mondragon: The growth and dynamics of the worker cooperative complex.* New York: ILR Press.

Wiemann, J. (1977). Explication and test of a model of communicative competence. *Human Communication Research, 3,* 195-213.

Wilson, A. (1990). *Participating in a participative management system: The role of active participation, organizational knowledge, and individual motivation in employee satisfaction and performance.* Unpublished dissertation, Purdue University, West Lafayette, IN.

Wofford, J., Gerloff, E., & Cummins, R. (1979). Group behavior and the communication process. In R. Cathcart & L. Samovar (Eds.), *Small group communication: A reader* (3rd ed.). Dubuque, IA: William C. Brown.

Wood, J., & Conrad, C. (1983). Paradox in the experiences of professional women. *Western Journal of Speech Communication, 47,* 305-322.

# Name Index

# Subject Index

# About the Author

**Cynthia Stohl** is Professor of Communication at Purdue University, West Lafayette, Indiana. Her research and teaching focus upon organizational and small group communication with a primary emphasis on the dynamic relationship among worker participation, communication networks, and global integration. Over the past 10 years, her papers have received several awards in the Organizational, Interpersonal, and Instructional Divisions of the International Communication Association and the Speech Communication Association. Her research on quality circles in New Zealand, semi-autonomous work groups in the United States, and the social and semantic networks of managers in the European Union has appeared in several journals including *Human Communication Research, Communication Monographs, Management Communication Quarterly*, and *Discourse & Society*, and the annual *Communication Yearbook*. She was the 1993 recipient of Purdue University's Charles B. Murphy Award for Outstanding Undergraduate Teaching. She has also taught organizational communication as part of the Purdue at Oxford program, Oxford, England, and has been a visiting teacher/scholar at the University of Aarhus, Denmark, and the University of Canterbury, Christchurch, New Zealand.